For Clyde,
my patient one.

Tarot of the Elves

including the novella
The Tarot of the Elves

By Mark McElroy
Cover image by Davide Corsi
Illustrations by Davide Corsi

First English Edition
First printing, 2007

Editing and book design:
Pietro Alligo, Riccardo Minetti

Printed in the EU

Lo Scarabeo S.r.l.
Via Cigna 110, 10155 - Torino - Italy
info@loscarabeo.com - www.loscarabeo.com

Printed by
Graf Art
Venaria - Torino

ISBN10 88-8395-646-X
ISBN 978-88-8395-646-1

Mark McElroy
Artwork by Davide Corsi

Tarot of the
ELVES

LO SCARABEO

INDEX

Author's Introduction
Mark McElroy, March 2007

Make no mistake: people take Elves very seriously.

As word circulated through the online Tarot community that I was creating the *Tarot of the Elves*, I received a great deal of email from people who feel a special bond with Elves.

In the minds of many, the work of J. R. R. Tolkien sets the standard for all things Elvish. Some Tolkien fans, in fact, had only one question: would the Elves in the *Tarot of the Elves* be based on Tolkien's concepts? If so, they wanted a copy immediately; if not, they warned, the deck would hold little or no interest for them. (In fact, one young man said he would feel led to "actively oppose the production of a deck ... unfaithful to Tolkien's universe"!)

Happily, I was also approached by more gentle souls, many of whom explained they had been seeing, speaking with, and interacting with Elves for most of their lives. Members of this group often distinguish between Elves (living, breathing members of a modern-day magical tribe) and "fantasy Elves" (fictional creatures frequently appearing in role-playing games, genre novels, and New Age art). These "friends of the Elves" consider their lives to be steeped in enchantment, and they assure me their experiences with the Elves are life-transforming.

Not long before this book went to press, I received a very kind letter from a representative of yet another group: an online organization dedicated to the articulation and practice of an Elven spiritual path. Some members claim to be Elves or descendants of Elves; others merely feel a strong affinity for all things Elvish. All, though, seemed quite sincere in their pursuit of their particular spiritual path ... and, of all those who contacted me with questions and concerns, they were at once the most polite and the most memorable.

I have deep respect and admiration for Tolkien's work, but as a writer and storyteller, I felt no obligation to borrow from his vividly realized world. I'm intrigued by the testimony of those who see and speak with Elves every day, but, as I am not one of these people, I could not create a deck from their perspective. I marvel at the creativity and boldness required to illuminate and adopt a spiritual path rooted in Elven culture, but as I am on another path, I am not the best person to communicate that faith to the world at large.

In the end, the only Elves I can introduce you to are the Elves who began to appear in my dreams, day and night, as I worked on the *Tarot of the Elves*: the Elves of New Alfheimr.

The Alfheimran Elves

At one point in the companion novel, *Velorl*, an Elven Priest, consults a diagram of "the twelve planets." This phrase surprised even me, popping up of its own volition. Upon reflection, it now makes sense to me that Alfheimran Elves may hail from a world other than our own. There's some even some precedent for this: Elven lore does refer to the Elves as "star people," and there are occasional suggestions that some Elves have left Earth for other worlds.

But, like so many people in our modern world, the Elves of New Alfheimr have lost their way. With each passing day, the well-worn Old Path loses ground to shiny, seductive technologies. The ancient stories are no longer told; as a result, the younger generation lacks a sense of place or purpose. A poisonous influence has overtaken their culture, and now the Elves of New Alfheimr are forgetting their legacy and identity.

In my mind, though, this does not, by any means, make the Elves of Alfheimr "lesser Elves." They've fallen, but, as a result, they now have the opportunity to rediscover themselves – but only if they are bold enough to respond to destiny's call.

Approached on their own merits, they have a great deal to teach us.

Why a Tarot of the Elves?

The lowly Tarot pack – now as easily acquired as a standard poker deck – is essentially a portable encyclopedia of myth and symbolism. When Tarot cards were created in Renaissance Italy, the mythic and Biblical references in the trump illustrations were widely recognized; today, the same cards appear "spooky" simply because contemporary audiences have little or no idea what these images mean.

Joseph Campbell recognized and popularized the idea that human societies use myths and legends to pass along values and expectations. Characters in myths, legends, and folk tales teach us how to act, how to respond when threatened, and what penalties await those who defy convention. Look at the heroes in any culture's myths, and you will see what traits are valued; in the villains, you will see what traits are despised.

Unfortunately, most Westerners (and, particularly, Americans) have grown up in a culturally illiterate society. Old stories are no longer told; once-familiar symbols have long been forgotten. Cut off from the well-spring of cultural wisdom, our society becomes increasingly detached, isolated, and violent.

We would do well, then, to reacquaint the general public with Tarot – because, when we do so, we are reconnecting people with a rich vein of insight and wisdom. *The Tarot of the Elves* seeks to make this easier by dressing up ancient knowledge in the bright, shiny clothes of a fantasy adventure. These cards are rooted in the myths and legends of the Alfheimran Elves ... but because the deck is true to the themes and structure of Tarot, it can also serve as a reintroduction to a vital part of our Western heritage.

Why a Companion Novel?

Tarot and Story have always been intertwined.

The figures appearing on the earliest Tarot cards were very likely inspired by the progression of characters in popular medieval "triumphal processions" – elaborate parades that brought moral tales to life and taught subtle lessons about the nature of the world. One of the earliest recorded uses for Tarot cards was a parlor game that involved composing stories about the characters on the trumps. When a Tarot reader reads the cards, he or she weaves the symbols into a story – a narrative the client can apply to his or her own situation.

In the process of developing the *Tarot of the Elves*, I found myself having to imagine the myths and legends of an entirely different culture ... *stories* that shaped the Elves'

awareness of their world and their place within it. As I began folding these stories into the structure of contemporary Tarot, I began to sense that they were something really special – a realization that was magnified when I saw the first dazzling illustrations David Corsi created based on my script for the deck.

Very early in the process, then, I realized I wanted to do more than offer this deck with the usual catalog of keywords and correspondences – and so I hit upon the idea of using a short novel as a way to draw people into the world of the *Tarot of the Elves*. Rather than tell the legends outright, I thought it might be interesting to create the character of Panopael, who, like the reader, is completely divorced from the world of the cards. During the course of the story, the reader shares her gradual insights, becoming familiar with the deck and its legends as the adventure progresses.

The companion novel, then, is your key to bringing the *Tarot of the Elves* to life. It is not required reading; the deck will function perfectly well when read on a purely intuitive basis. However, if you take the time to live through the stories behind each card, you will find that the *Tarot of the Elves* will speak with a level of insight and degree of wisdom that will surprise and delight you.

A Truly "Novel" Way to Learn Tarot

In addition, the companion novel offers readers a unique opportunity to learn to read and handle a Tarot deck. For beginners, and especially for those who like to learn by experience (instead of by memorization or lecture), reading the companion book can be a pleasant and effective introduction to the cards.

For more experienced Tarot readers, the companion novel reinforces the fact that every story (including every novel, television show, movie, song, work of art, and human life) embodies and reflects to some degree the steady progression from the innocence of The Fool to the enlightenment of The World.

As you follow Panopael's adventures, pay close attention to her interaction with the cards and ask yourself these questions:

• How does Panopael respond to the cards at first? What mistakes does she make? What assumptions hinder her progress?

• How is Panopael's deck structured? What's the point of this structure? What are the benefits of it?

• How does Panopael read a card? How does she determine the meaning of a card? What role do keywords, symbols, or stories play in her interpretation? What role does intuition play? How does her process change throughout the course of the book?

• To what extent are Panopael's initial impressions and first interpretations always correct? How does she "fine tune" her interpretations to arrive at more precise readings?

• How do the cards interact with Panopael? What do the cards "do" in a reading? How does Panopael respond? When you are working with the cards ... how will you respond to behaviors like these?

• To what extent are the messages from Panopael's cards symbolic? To what extent are they literal? What might this have to say about the nature of messages from Tarot in general?

As Panopael experiences the cards of the Major Arcana by living through their story, each card literally becomes a chapter in her adventure.

• How do the events and themes in the chapters reflect the meanings assigned to the corresponding Major Cards? What phrases – in the text and in the mouths of the characters – might help illuminate the meaning of each card?

• What does Panopael learn about the four-suited Minor Cards? How are these different from the Majors? How might that difference figure in the way you read and interpret the cards?

• What hints are there in the story with regard to the nature of Tarot? By the end of the story, how would Panopael answer the question, "How do Tarot cards work?"

• What does this story teach that Tarot is good for? Under what circumstances do you see Tarot being used?

• Based on what you see in the story, what qualities or habits would you say might enhance a reader's ability to work with the cards? What qualities or habits might interfere with a reader's ability to read with precision?

• Based on what you see in the story, where would you say the "magic" in Tarot's remarkable ability to present the past, reflect the present, and predict the future lies?

• By design, the reading at the end of the story is presented ... but not interpreted. Based on what you know from reading the book, what would you say the reading indicates? What information gives you faith in your interpretation of that reading?

Finally, like Panopael, you may find that your study of Tarot alters your sense of self and your vision of your place in the Universe. You will come to see how certain kinds of events are very likely to give way to others. You will come to recognize certain people and certain energies, and, as you interact with them, you will receive strong intuitive impressions about what to do and what not to do ... even when your cards are not in your hands.

Book One:

Dystopia

Chapter One

Panopael Mallir sat alone in the back seat of her father's water carriage. Her father, Filhardil, still angry, sat up front.

Filhardil was tall and thin, even for an Elf. He wore his hair in the new style, pulled back into a severe, shiny ponytail. His long black cloak, embroidered with Governor Narnilor's official seal, made him look even taller and thinner. As the carriage churned its way across the choppy lake between New Alfheimr and the Old City, the turbulence made Filhardil's lean form weave back and forth, back and forth.

He looks like a water snake, Panopael thought. *Poking up from the lakebed and luring little fish to their doom.*

Filhardil turned and glared at her. Panopael glanced away. Had Governor Narnilor given her father one of those boxes – a box for reading minds? She couldn't be sure ... but just in case, she filled her head with an old nursery rhyme.

Her father cleared his throat and faced front again.

As they drew closer to the Old City, the rain began. Hard, fat drops smacked the carriage's transparent see-shell windows; soon, the downpour reduced the whole world to shades of gray. Panopael peered out, but saw nothing but her own reflection. Bored, she breathed on the see-shell to fog it, then used a fingernail to trace the familiar lines of her face – the limp dark hair, the almond-shaped eyes, the sharp Elven chin.

A sudden lurch to one side marred her efforts. As the carriage left the lake and roared up on land, its eight legs unfolded and scrambled for purchase on the muddy bank. Their progress kicked up great sheets of black sand until they reached the Ring Road; at that point, the carriage filled with the clatter of armored legs on cobblestones.

"Gather your things," her father said. "We're almost at her house."

"I have my own life," Panopael said. "Friends and parties."

Filhardil snorted.

Panopael rolled her eyes. "People ask, 'What are you doing?' I have to say, 'Going to my grandmother's.' It's embarrassing."

"She's your grandmother."

"But I *hate* her," Panopael said.

"So do I. But she's your grand-mother, and you'll spend the day with her."

"You don't care that she's my grandmother," Panopael said. "You just care what people would say if I *didn't* go see her."

Filhardil didn't deny this; he merely shrugged.

"I won't speak to her," Panopael said.

"You could do *me* that favor."

"I'll write a note, claim to run away, and hide in the attic. She'll call Enforcers. The story will be all over New Alfheimr."

Filhardil glanced back at her. "Just get to it, Panopael. What do you want?"

Panopael beamed. "A party for me. With only food I like! And I can invite who I please – no boring people. And no one who still does magic."

Filhardil nodded approvingly. "Shunning the magic users?"

Panopael shrugged. "Magic's so ... Old City."

"So Old City!" Filhardil laughed. "When I tell Narnilor that, he'll promote me on the spot."

As they reached the heart of Old City, the streets became increasingly narrow. At times, the sides of the carriage scraped the walls of passing houses, gouging scars in the ancient stone. If Filhardil noticed, he didn't care.

As the carriage scurried through the Circle of the Well, beggars risked life and limb to draw near the vehicle's scissoring legs, tap on its shell, and ask for alms. Her father's fingers danced over the switches up front, darkening the see-shell windows, but Panopael could still hear the beggar's pitiful cries: "Ooon! Ooon! Oooooon!"

The carriage shifted suddenly to the right, sending three beggars sprawling. Up in the driver's seat, Filhardil chuckled. "Elves begging," he said. "It's disgusting."

"Someone should do something," Panopael said.

They said nothing more until the carriage lurched to a halt in front of Grandmother Taemerl's house: a steep, three-story affair built of dull Old City stone, squeezed in among hundreds of others just like it.

"Out," Filhardil said.

"What time will you pick me up tonight?"

"Out."

Defeated, Panopael gathered her case and her books. The carriage's shell stretched open, and Panopael stepped out onto the street. The odors of the Old City rose up around her: seafood, garbage, the grassy stench of willowbeer. Panopael made a face. "If you don't keep your promise about the party, I'll become a beggar!"

The carriage shuddered. Its shell snapped shut. It clattered away.

* * * * *

Panopael hated everything about Grandmother Taemerl's house.

Everyone knew that proper, modern lighting demanded fusetubes and spotbrights. Even so, Grandmother Taemerl still used candles and pungent oil lamps. Instead of self-cleaning plexisteel, the walls of her house were chilly stone, covered with cracked plaster. Thankfully, most of the walls were hidden behind worn draperies, splintery cabinets, and rickety shelves.

Plants – creepy ones, with leathery leaves and spiky vines – cascaded from random pots. Every table and chair held boxes of bottles: vials of spices, powders, and foul-smelling liquids.

"The woman lives in a rummage shop," Filhardil often said – and, as much as doing so galled her, Panopael had to agree.

And then, of course, there was Grandmother Taemerl herself.

Grandmother Taemerl was embarrassingly elderly. She refused to dye her stringy hair, preferring instead to twist it into long and complicated old-style braids. She refused to use seastinger oil to tighten the skin of her face and hands, so her flesh was etched with deep wrinkles. And while virtually everyone else – even here, in the Old City – preferred to spend the evening gorging on split-root or guzzling willowbeer, Grandmother Taemerl sat at home, alone, eating boiled vegetables and reading books.

It wasn't that she couldn't afford luxuries. Filhardil sent lots of money ... but Grandmother gave it away.

But never to me, Panopael thought. With the door bolted behind her, she leaned forward into the shadows of her grandmother's receiving room. "Taemerl?"

A sudden, morbid fantasy popped into Panopael's head. What if Taemerl were dead? What if the old witch were upstairs, right now, stiff in her bed, with her eyeballs collapsed back into her skull?

What if I have to spend an entire day alone here with a corpse?

Even as that thought gave her gooseflesh, something in the shadows lurched forward.

Chapter Two

Panopael jumped – but it was just Taemerl.

The old Elf dropped a case of dried mushrooms onto a pile of other boxes; the resulting flurry of dust had her fanning the air and coughing. Taemerl was bent over, hands on her knees, hacking, when she spotted Panopael.

Taemerl squinted. "Compulsory visit, hmm?"

Panopael winced. "I have studying."

Taemerl straightened up, bracing her back with her hands. "Real studying ... or that worthless poop they teach in New City schools?"

The points of Panopael's ears turned red. "Father sends his love."

Taemerl grunted. "Your father's a fool, sucking up to the likes of Governor Narnilor."

"Narnilor's taking the Elves into a new age," Panopael said, quoting her father.

"Narnilor's taking the Elves straight to hell," Taemerl said. The old woman drew a breath, paused, then narrowed her eyes. "How did you get here?"

"Governor Narnilor gave Father a brand new water carriage."

Taemerl rolled her eyes and threw up her hands. "Elves! Running around in mechanical crab shells instead of traveling by magic!"

"Technology shows our mastery over nature," Panopael said, quoting her father again.

Taemerl shook her fist at her granddaughter. "Magic shows our *oneness* with nature." She froze in place, her hand relaxing slowly. "And you're playing me, exactly the way your father does." The old Elf sighed. "Will we do what we always do? Retreat to different parts of the house?"

"I have studying," Panopael said again. "History."

"History?"

Panopael squeezed her eyes shut. "Narnilor the Eighth: current governor and father of the New Age of Prosperity. Edicts of Progress: restricted magic and commissioned the construction of New Alfheimr. Anniston Theftamil: mother of weather control." Her eyes opened. "Father says if I learn enough, I'll get a water carriage of my own."

Taemerl spat on the floor. "Like most Elves these days, you know a lot, but you understand very little."

Panopael blinked. "What?"

"You play with the pieces but ignore the puzzle." Taemerl clenched her fists and crossed the room. As she approached Panopael, the tables and boxes in her path rearranged themselves, clearing a path. "Why did the New Age of Prosperity put beggars on the streets? How does trading our magical heritage for buzzing black boxes equal progress? And how do perpetually sunny skies in New Alfheimr impact the rest of the world?"

Slowly and deliberately, Panopael lifted one of her schoolbooks and opened the cover. "Magic's old fashioned."

Without warning, the book in her hand shuddered, becoming an ornate wooden box.

Startled, Panopael tossed the box away; it hit the floor with an audible crack. The lid, decorated with jewels and gold wire, snapped off, releasing a cascade of cards. Some landed face up, revealing glimpses of brightly colored illustrations: spiders, yellow flowers, shiny blades, a pool of water.

Taemerl folded her arms. "Now you've done it."

Panopael's heart raced – first with shock, and then with anger. "*I've* done it? *You* did it!"

"I just stood here."

"You magicked it, and you know it," Panopael said, gesturing at the mess. She glanced up at her grandmother. "Its like the first line of the Edicts says: *Magic works against an orderly world.*"

Taemerl snorted. "Order's overrated."

"You could have just handed me the box, like a normal person. You could have–" Panopael, pointing to the floor, abruptly stopped talking. The broken box and the cards were gone.

Taemerl, looking smug, stepped forward and offered Panopael the jeweled box – whole and unbroken.

Panopael put her hands behind her back. "I have studying."

"You do have things you need to learn," Taemerl said. With that, the old Elf flickered and vanished. Above Panopael's head, the ceiling creaked; Grandmother had magicked herself upstairs.

"Old fashioned!" Panopael said loudly. Surrounded by clutter, she stood there for several seconds, straining to hear an answer. When none came, she sighed, shrugged, and stooped to gather the rest of her schoolbooks.

In their place sat the bejeweled box.

Panopael stamped her foot. "Rude!"

Again: no answer.

Fuming, the young Elf flounced across the room and threw herself into the only chair not covered with boxes, books, or bottles. She swung her feet. She shifted in her seat. She listened to the ticking of Taemerl's mantle clock.

Bored, she turned her attention to the table beside her seat – and there, once again, was the bejeweled box.

Panopael sighed. "Fine. You want me to look at the box? I'll look at the box."

She lifted the box – it was heaver than she expected – and placed it in her lap. It was made of warm, polished wood; the surface was smooth and soft to the touch. By contrast, the lid was rough, festooned with tiny gold plates and fat red and green jewels. The center of the lid was dominated by an elaborate design: twenty-two mother-of-pearl chips arranged in a circle around a huge, clear stone.

"It is beautiful," Panopael admitted – and then, with a rush of pleasure, it occurred to her that the box might be a present. Grinning, she ran eager fingers around the edges, found the catch, and lifted the lid.

When she looked inside, she screamed.

Chapter Three

Panopael threw the box to the floor.

Rearing up out of it was a huge spider, larger than either of Panopael's hands. Its fat abdomen and jointed legs bristled with brown fur, and its eight moist eyes glistened like polished pinheads.

Panopael drew her legs up into the chair. The spider, sensing movement, crouched and flexed its mandibles, disgorging a thick, sticky strand of venom.

Panopael froze, her heart hammering in her ears. She could rake everything off the tabletop onto the floor, crushing the spider beneath the mess. She could take her chances and kick the box away, but the spider could jump onto her leg as she did so. She could call out for Taemerl – but that would give the crafty old Elf too much satisfaction.

And then, out of nowhere, a new thought popped into her head: *Where did the cards in the box go?*

She frowned, struggling to recreate a mental image of the broken box and scattered deck. In her mind's eye, she reviewed each card: one with a sword, one with a daffodil, one with water...

Hadn't one of the cards featured a picture of a spider just like this one?

Panopael took a deep breath, then leaned down to give the creature a closer look.

The spider responded by crouching lower, wriggling its forelegs, and hissing.

Panopael gritted her teeth and refused to pull back. Now, bending down, she could see a level of detail she'd missed before. The edges of the spider shimmered; the lines of the legs and the edges of its abdomen were blurry and indistinct.

Panopael raised her hand. With a firm and decisive motion, she swiped at the spider – or tried to. Even as her hand came near the beast, the spider grew less distinct. As her fingers passed through its transparent body, she saw a brief flash of light and heard a faint pop. With that, the spider was gone.

In its place was now a card featuring a drawing of the spider – detailed and colorful, but definitely flat and lifeless. As Panopael watched, the drawing flowed to life; the spider receded, and Panopael could see blades of lush green grass surrounding it. The image receded even further, and Panopael could now see that the spider in the grass was crawling quite close to someone's bare ankles. An instant later, she could see the owner of the ankles – a handsome young Elf with long, flowing hair.

When the picture froze again, Panopael lifted the card to peer at the final result. In the illustration, the handsome young Elf reclined against mossy rocks in the middle of a grassy meadow. Neither he nor his sleeping dog noticed the hateful spider crawling in the grass; instead, the bare-chested young man amused himself by encouraging butterflies to light on the tips of his fingers. In the background, in the shadows of a powerful oak, a smiling Elven maiden looked on, but the Elf was too caught up in his own game to notice her.

"Ignoring her," Panopael murmured. "The way everyone ignores me."

Most puzzling, though, was the caption at the bottom of the card: *The Fool.* Panopael frowned, trying to relate the words to the image. Was the Elf a fool for not spotting the spider? Or was the maiden a fool for thinking she might eventually get the young Elf's attention?

The sound of a noisy and deliberate descent down the stairs broke the girl's concentration. Panopael, though, refused to look up; even when Taemerl drew close, the girl kept her head down. "Walking down stairs? Did you run out of magic?"

Taemerl spat on the floor. "Run *out* of magic? Elves *are* magic. You've just forgotten it." She nodded at the box in Panopael's hands. "And to know so much about history, you don't seem to know the legend of Prince Alberich and his wife, the oracle Ellyll."

"I have more important things to learn."

Taemerl laughed. "Like learning how to vomit?"

Panopael's eyes widened. "What?"

"They tell you the questions. They tell you the answers. You swallow it all. You vomit it up on command." Taemerl crossed the room and put a bony finger under Panopael's chin. "Tell me, brilliant daughter of my brilliant son: can you do more than vomit?"

Despite her best efforts, Panopael giggled. "Yes."

The older woman grinned. "I thought as much, especially when you passed the spider test."

Panopael pulled away. "I knew the spider was fake."

Without bothering to move the papers stacked on the cushions, Taemerl plopped down in one of the overstuffed chairs. "Do you always scream at fake spiders?"

Panopael gazed down at the card in her hand. "Magic box, magic spider. It doesn't take a genius."

"Or perhaps it does," Taemerl said. "Old Brownie has scared many an unworthy soul away, and yet ... here you are. So: what do you think of Prince Alberich?"

Panopael wandered over to her grandmother's chair and wriggled up onto the armrest. "Why do they call him a Fool?"

"For the same reason I might call you one."

Panopael made a face. "That's not very nice."

Taemerl smiled. "The truth, Panopael, isn't always nice, but smart people still prefer it." With one long fingernail, she tapped the card. "There's more to being a Fool than you think. Now, read your grandmother a story, will you?"

Panopael turned the card over. "There aren't any words."

Taemerl closed her eyes. "For all of his years on Earth, young Prince Alberich enjoyed a life of total leisure. His father, wise King Oberon, Master of the Four Implements, guided the Elven people in all material matters; his mother, Queen Priestess Alva, served the people as their spiritual guide. Alberich, though, proved more handsome than hard-working. Even after his marriage to the lovely Ellyll, and even after she became pregnant with his child, the selfish Prince still chose daydreaming over getting things done." Her eyes snapped open. "Now you."

Panopael stuck out her tongue. "Vomited that out, did you?"

"If so, I'm sure an original story from Panopael Millar will be superior."

Panopael looked down at the card. "One day, when he least expected it, the gods sent Prince Alberich a challenge in the form of a hairy spider."

"Did Alberich scream like a little girl?"

"He almost didn't even see it," Panopael said. "But at the last minute, he was clever enough to know a trick when he saw one."

Taemerl pointed to the sleeping dog. "What did his instincts tell him about the spider?"

"His instincts were useless, because nothing had prepared him for something this unusual." Panopael squinted, drawing the card closer. "That's why the dog's asleep."

"Perceptive," Taemerl said. "Tell me more."

Panopael bristled. "Is this another test?"

"Everything is."

Panopael sighed. "He's very young. He's beautiful, but he's selfish." She pointed to the butterflies. "He flits from task to task like a butterfly flitting from flower to flower." She pointed to the maiden in the background. "People love him, and are willing to support him, but he takes all this for granted." She pointed to the spider. "But all of that is about to change. Is that a good enough story for you?"

Panopael looked up. Her question hung in the air, unanswered.

She was no longer sitting in her grandmother's house.

Book Two:

The Tarot of the Elves

Chapter Zero

> **Trump 0 – The Fool.** "Prince Alberich lived an insulated life of leisure." *Folly, inexperience, potential. Beginners and beginnings. Sincerity over practicality, dreams over achievements. Creative leaps, leaps of faith, or an optimistic refusal to think critically.*

Panopael sat very still, taking stock of her situation.

Above her: a cloudless sky. Around her: massive oaks, their limbs thick with whispering leaves. The clearing in which she sat was carpeted with knee-high yellow grasses; monarch butterflies played among the tallest of the blades.

Panopael sat on sun-warmed rocks. The limestone base, paired with the upright stones behind her back, formed a comfortable seat – as comfortable, in fact, as the padded chair in her grandmother's house.

"Taemerl?"

Insects buzzed and blackbirds chattered.

She ran an unsteady hand over the surface of the limestone; it felt perfectly solid. She peered at the bobbing grasses and shifting leaves, but saw no trace of the tell-tale shimmer that had tipped her off to the illusory spider.

Thoughts of the spider drew her attention back to the card in her hand. It looked completely ordinary, now: a picture of young Prince Alberich, sitting in a lush meadow, reclining against sunlit stones –

Panopael's heart skipped a beat. *This* lush meadow ... *these* sunlit stones. She was in the card ... alone.

Panopael stood, half-expecting the ground to give way beneath her. When it didn't, she made her way up a gentle slope to the spot where, on the card, Alberich's wife, Ellyll, stood beneath the great oak tree.

In the distance, she saw gleaming marble buildings scattered among green hills. She recognized the domed ceilings and blunt towers of the Old City immediately – but never in her life had the Old City looked so clean and new.

Beyond the Old City, she could see sunlight glinting off the placid waters of Lake Daelamr. But on the far side of the lake, where the green skyscrapers and vermillion banners of New Alfheimr belonged, there was only a vast plain of purple grasses.

Above Panopael's head, the oak leaves rustled. Despite the bright sun, there was a chilly undercurrent in the breeze. She glanced up at the sky and frowned. Before long, the sun would kiss the peaks of the Western Range – and then she would be out here, alone, in the dark.

Fuming, Panopael walked back down to the sun-warmed rocks. She was telling herself that Taemerl had no right to strand her here – wherever here was – when she spotted something familiar on the limestone seat.

There, gleaming in the sunlight, was the ornate wooden box that had started it all.

Panopael sighed. "If I smash this, I guess it'll just reappear?" She didn't wait for an answer; she didn't expect any. Instead, she stood as far as she could from the box and, with great care, opened the lid.

Nothing happened. Panopael, still keeping her distance, peered inside … but all she could see inside was a deck of card. Holding her breath, Panopael lifted these from the box, but her caution proved unnecessary. The cards remained cards, and mundane cards at that.

The card at the top of the pack was completely different from the one Panopael still held in her right hand. On it, a swarthy, dark-skinned Elf juggled a half-circle of glowing runes. A young boy, mesmerized, looked on and applauded. The title of the card – The Magician – didn't strike Panopael as especially helpful. The red-robed man looked more like a juggler than a magician. Worse, the bag at his feet, stuffed with what looked like antiques, actually made him look like a peddler.

Or a thief.

Panopael blinked. Where had *that* idea come from? She paused, waiting to see if any other words would pop, unbidden, into her head. Several seconds later, already bored, she gave up, put all the cards back in the box, and hopped down.

Panopael took a deep breath, clutched the box to her chest, and started walking toward the Old City. She hadn't walked far before she came upon a wide, flat road that made progress easy. Though she remained alert – she half-expected Taemerl to jump out at any moment – she found herself almost enjoying the journey.

An hour passed, and then two. Panopael's feet hurt worse with every step. Why wasn't anyone else on this road? And how much farther away could the Old City be? As shadows around her grew longer, she felt her spirit wilting. Weary and worried, Panopael plopped down on the side of the road and scanned the horizon.

Nothing she saw gave her comfort. The butterflies – her only companions – had deserted her. The sky – bright blue earlier in the afternoon – had turned to gray steel. Ahead of her, the road stretched on, and the distant city buildings looked no closer. She felt like crying.

And then, far away, but definitely not a trick of the light, she saw a rippling black form in the middle of the road.

Panopael squinted, blinking back tears. At first, she thought she might be seeing a flag: a length of ebony fabric, fluttering in the breeze. But as the smudge drew closer, she could make out more detail: a hood, broad shoulders, a flowing cape.

An Elf!

Panopael's initial response – to stand and wave, to call out, to run toward the only other person she'd seen since her arrival – quickly gave way to caution. The approaching figure might be a friend … and he might not be.

Panopael nibbled her lower lip and considered hiding in the roadside grasses. But it was too late; up ahead, the black-robed man had stopped in the middle of the highway.

He was staring right at her.

Chapter One

Trump I - The Magician. "Dokkalfar, the Dark Elf, poses as a conjurer to steal the Four Implements." *Capability, power, deception. Illusions and visions. Becoming a channel for divine will. Mastery of skills, and the application of those skills to reach a desired goal.*

Panopael thought fast. She shifted the box under her right arm; if she had to, she could lob it at the stranger like a rock. It was only a wooden box – but it was heavy enough, and if it struck home, it would hurt.

He remained in the middle of the road, unmoving.

Panopael took a deep breath, clamped her teeth together, and started walking forward. At almost the same time, the other Elf resumed progress, too – heading directly for her.

Panopael kept moving. Soon, her sensitive ears picked up a jangling noise – metallic objects jostling against each other. As the man drew even closer, she identified the source of the sound: a pink fabric satchel, half-hidden in the folds of his cloak.

As the distance between them dwindled, Panopael could make out other details, despite the failing light. The approaching figure had hair as dark as Panopael's, but worn long and loose, with single braids framing either side of his face. Beneath thick brows, his black eyes sparkled like smooth river stones. His complexion was much darker than usual, and his lips were a bit too wide for his face.

Gooseflesh prickled on her arms as she recognized him: the Magician from Taemerl's mysterious pack of cards.

When he was no more than a few strides away, the Magician stopped again, dropped his satchel, and put his hands on his hips.

Panopael's instincts told her to run; even so, she hesitated. Whoever this Magician turned out to be, he was the only other person she'd seen since her arrival. With the skies growing darker and the air growing colder by the minute, she decided to remain cautious ... but hope for the best. "Excuse me," she said, trying to sound confident. "I've been walking for hours, but not getting anywhere. Is this the road to the Old City?"

The Magician tossed back his hood and smiled.

A Dark Elf! The realization made Panopael shiver. Back in New Alfheimr, there were no Dark Elves – except, of course, in stories. Dark Elves were the stuff of bad Harvest tales – swarthy stock villains for scaring small children. Dark Elves, the legend said, were always born twins, but the mother and father always devoured the weaker of the two. Dark Elves, the stories warned, stole children's pets, skinned them alive, and turned the hides into grisly puppets.

When the Dark Elf spoke, his voice was rich and deep – the voice of a seasoned warrior. "Run back to Volundr, little one, and share this news: my task is complete, and the Implements are coming."

Dark Elf or not ... he's the only person I've met so far. Panopael cleared her throat. "I can't run back to a place I've never head of. I'm trying to get to New Alfheimr. Do you know the way or not?"

The Dark Elf took three strides forward, grabbed Panopael by the shoulders, and shook her. "Not even Volundr's own messenger should address the Hand of God with such disrespect. Now stop yammering and take my reply to your master!"

Panopael's squirmed out of his grasp. "You touch me one more time, and my father will bring Narnilor's Enforcers down on you so hard, not even the hands of the gods will protect you!"

The Dark Elf stood and stomped his foot. "Are you simple-minded? Have you been chewing spinweed? Why would Volundr choose such a –" The Magician's jaw dropped, and his eyes narrowed down to black slits. "You're not the messenger."

"I'm just lost. I'm just trying–"

The Magician lunged forward; before Panopael could run, he had her by the hair. As she squealed in terror, he pulled her face closer to his. "You're not even a Dark Elf." He gave her hair a yank. "What's your clan?"

Panopael burst into tears. "I don't have a clan!"

The Dark Elf abruptly released her. "Dark hair, but light skin," he said, his upper lip curling. "A half-breed." He glanced down at the box in her hands. "And a thief."

Panopael's scalp throbbed. She stumbled backward, putting distance between them. "The box is mine."

The Magician took a step in her direction. "You stole that box, didn't you? And you killed the messenger who carried it."

"It's my grandmother's box!"

The Magician snickered. "Yours ... or your grandmother's? Keep your story straight, you filthy mongrel." He reached inside his cape, producing a sharp hunting knife. "I can gut a harpdeer with three quick strokes. So do you give me box ... or will I take it, along with your hide?"

Panopael felt faint. The box might be her only way home; if she gave it up, she might get trapped in a strange and frightening world. A part of her wanted to doubt that the Dark Elf would kill her ... but her scalp, still sore, reminded her that he wouldn't hesitate to cause her pain.

And then, in that very instant, she noticed something she had over-looked before: the Magician's knife, from the leather-wrapped handle to the tip of the cruel blade, was out-lined in an odd, shimmering blur.

Just like Taemerl's spider!

Panopael hugged the box to her chest and stepped forward. "Then gut me."

The Dark Elf's nostrils flared. "I'll slice you from belly to chin. I'll split you like a piece of rotten fruit. Is that box worth dying for, you stupid little half-breed?"

Summoning all her courage, she took a deep breath ... shifted Taemerl's box to her left hand ... and grabbed the Dark Elf's blade with her right.

Chapter Two

Panopael's hand passed through the blade, closing on empty air. The knife rippled, then popped like a bubble.

To Panopael's surprise, the Magician responded with little more than a shrug. "Brave little half-breed. Keep your box." He stepped back, smiling a smile that did not touch his eyes. "Did you say you were going to the city?"

Panopael, still terrified, merely nodded.

"I know just the place," the Magician said. He waved his hands and, in a deep and frightening voice, uttered a phrase in an unfamiliar tongue.

Panopael felt a sudden surge of heat and pressure ... and then, an instant later, she felt nothing at all.

* * * * *

Somewhere, someone screamed.

Panopael's eyes opened wide. Aside from playground pranks, she hadn't had much experience with screams. This one, though, was a scream of pure agony.

Still disoriented, Panopael started searching for Taemerl's wooden box. When she found it, she leaned back against the smooth stone wall and shook her head. Where was she?

Looking up, she could see a distant ceiling: a dome, with a circle of blue sky visible through the center.

Slowly, her eyes adjusted to the gloom. She was in a temple of some kind – a round room with tall columns spaced evenly along its perimeter. Panopael gasped. The Oraculum! She'd been here before, on school trips to the Old City.

She remembered the Teacher's obvious distaste with the place. "Pre-Narnilor," the Teacher had said. "Terrible time in our history. All magic – no technology. Not even any hybrids. Barbaric."

"What did people do here?" Panopael had asked.

The Teacher had frowned. "Ancients believed a Priestess could see the future. Pure garbage, of course, but people took religion seriously then." She had pointed to the throne between the black and white columns. "Woman sat there. People asked questions. She made up answers."

"Was the Priestess ever right?" Panopael had asked.

"That won't be on the test," the Teacher had said. "Oraculum: a temple of prediction. That's all you need to know."

The scream came again, snapping her out of her reverie. Whatever was going on, Panopael wanted no part of it. She stood and moved as quietly as possible along the curved wall, heading for the entrance arch. She was only a few steps shy of it when she spotted a detail that stopped her in her tracks.

Where the gaping maw of the entrance should have been, Panopael saw two massive wooden doors. More than forty feet high, they were made of polished blushwood and decorated with bright jewels and golden runes. A huge beam, elaborately carved and studded with gemstones, lay across them, preventing anyone from outside from getting in ...and preventing anyone inside from getting out.

Panopael was an excellent student, and she recalled with perfect clarity what the Teacher had said as the class left the Oraculum: "The temple used to be sealed, of course. You can see scars in the portal where the hinges were, and scrapes on the floor where the doors used to swing inward. Superstitious locals plastered the blushwood with expensive doo-dads, and thieves broke down the doors and made away with the loot. Of course, that was more than two thousand years ago."

"Taemerl's magicked me backward in time," Panopael murmured aloud.

The dome of the Oraculum magnified her words; she might as well have shouted. The temple erupted with the noise of sudden response: startled cries, the percussion of rapid footsteps, the unmistakable metallic clatter of weapons being drawn.

* * * * *

Despite Panopael's protests, a team of Enforcers dragged her past frightened onlookers and dropped her in the center of the Oraculum.

The Tarot of the Elves

There, a slender young man in white robes kneeled on a dais between two stone columns, sobbing. With a jolt, Panopael recognized him as Prince Alberich.

Another Elf – a woman older than Alberich – lay on her side in a pool of bright blood. It oozed from a cruel wound in her belly, puddled on the chilly floor, and soaked into a parchment scroll near the dead woman's knees.

Alberich climbed unsteadily to his feet. He pointed to Panopael with a trembling finger. "Do you realize what you've done?"

Panopael, horrified, could barely speak. "I'm not ... I didn't ..."

Alberich lurched forward and grabbed her by the shoulders. "You filthy Dark Elf scum! You've murdered my mother!"

"Enough!"

It was only one word, but the voice behind it carried obvious authority. Alberich let go of Panopael and backed away.

From out of the darkness, a willowy form emerged: a tall Elf, with long golden hair, fair skin, and white robes. Though her mouth was set into a firm, straight line, there was something kind about her overall expression. Her belly was swollen with pregnancy; still, she moved with silent grace. Panopael recognized her immediately: Alberich's wife, Ellyll.

Ellyll placed a hand on Alberich's shoulder, lingering there only a moment before turning her gaze on Panopael. "I apologize. My husband's mad with grief." She walked toward Panopael, taking slow, deliberate steps. "Among our people, the Priestess is empowered to practice divination – to serve as an oracle, parting the veil of secrecy to see What Truly Is. The murder of our Priestess is more than the murder of our Queen – it is an attempt to silence the Voice of Truth."

"I didn't kill anyone," Panopael said. "I'm just lost, and I want to go home."

Ellyll was now no more than an arm's length away. "My name is Ellyll. My husband is the son of the Priestess. Now, her duties fall to me. My Second Sight could tell me what happened here, but using it risks my baby's life ... so I'll ask questions. You will give answers. If you lie, I will know. Understand?"

"You get to say whether I'm telling the truth?"

"Yes."

Panopael shrugged. "Then I hope you're not the murderer."

A ghost of a smile played at the corners of Ellyll's lips. "Who are you?"

"Panopael Mallir."

Ellyll studied Panopael's face and hair. "Are you a Dark Elf?"

"There's no such thing as Dark Elves where I come from," Panopael said. "People are light and dark and everything in between."

Ellyll narrowed her eyes. "That must be wonderful."

"It's home. I want to get back."

"How did you get here?"

"I was on the road outside the Old City. I met a Magician who called himself The Hand of God. He thought I was a messenger from Volundr."

"Volundr isn't a place," Ellyll said. "It's an old word for demon."

Panopael shrugged. "He told me to run back to Volundr and say the task was complete. When I didn't understand, he tried to steal my grandmother's box ... and somehow sent me here."

Ellyll frowned. "Your grandmother's box?"

Panopael hesitated, but passed the box to Ellyll.

Ellyll opened it and removed the cards. "What are these?"

Panopael struggled to come up with an explanation, then drew inspiration from the room around her. "An old-fashioned oracle – Tarot cards."

"A divinatory tool," Ellyll said. She chose a card at random and glanced at the image.

Panopael leaned in closer and peered down at the card. "It's a picture of your husband," Panopael said. "The Fool."

The crowd gasped, but Ellyll smiled. She returned the card to the deck and drew another. "This one?"

Panopael swallowed hard. "It's called the Priestess. But she's been murdered, and your husband is kneeling beside her ... just like he was a few minutes ago."

Ellyll put the cards away. "I have one last question, Panopael. Did you have anything to do with the murder of Queen Priestess Alva?"

Panopael shook her head. "No, m'am."

"Panopael ... you're telling the truth."

Panopael's shoulders slumped with relief.

"These cards have an odor – cedar and rosewater. That's a sign of powerful magic, protecting the cards and the person who carries them." Ellyll sniffed. "You, on the other hand, smell of camphor and sulfur – a Dark Elf transport spell." She turned to face her husband and the other onlookers. "This girl was dropped here in hopes we would mistake her for the murderer."

A scar-faced Enforcer stepped forward. "We mustn't waste time. The murderer may be the magician on the Lake Road."

Ellyll turned to Panopael. "Do you trust me?"

With something like surprise, Panopael realized that she did. "Yes."

"I have obligations to attend to. Are you willing to go with one of my closest personal attendants to a safe place until I can find a way to get you home?"

Panopael nodded.

"Very well." Ellyll clapped twice, and a young woman stepped forward. "Panopael, this is my handmaiden ... Taemerl."

Chapter Three

The handmaiden called Taemerl was perhaps ten summers older than Panopael. Like Panopael's grandmother, this woman wore her hair in long, elaborate braids and held her pointed chin high. The more Panopael studied the eyebrows, the delicate nose, and the high cheekbones, the more she became convinced that, somehow, this Taemerl was hers.

"Grandmother?"

The other woman said nothing.

Near the entrance, a half-dozen men took hold of thick cables. Pulling down again and again, they turned unseen gears and opened the massive doors. Attendants encircled Ellyll and Alberich, whisking them outside. Other guards formed a tight circle around the central platform, protecting the body of the fallen Queen Priestess.

"When my father hears that you magicked me back in time—"

Without warning, Taemerl gave the younger girl a quick, firm slap across the face.

Panopael's eyes bulged. "No hitting!"

Taemerl bent down and, with lightning-quick hands, she snatched the Tarot box from Panopael's hands. "I'll have this back. At the safehouse, you'll tell me who you really are."

"You know who I am!"

Taemerl's pleasant expression never wavered, but she raised her right hand again, ready to deliver another sharp slap. "Shut your yap."

Panopael did exactly that. Soon after, Taemerl steered Panopael through the archway and into the bustling streets.

*****

Though bursting with questions, Panopael was soon mesmerized by the sights and sounds of Alfheimr.

On this corner, a baker hawked cinnamon-butter daycakes. Across the street, women bartered for bolts of shimmering cloth. Shopkeepers hung spheres of cheese above open racks of citrus fruits and mustard greens. Elders – their heads shaved, their robes impossibly white – walked the streets without fear of persecution from Narnilor's Progressive Guard.

The stench of magic was everywhere. Washwomen hurried through the Circle of the Well, followed by bobbing buckets of water. A food vendor snapped his fingers, bringing soups to an instant boil. Older women, their morning strolls complete, vanished, leaving no trace but the scent of camphor.

Taemerl led Panopael across a familiar cobbled street to the doorway of a house she would have recognized anywhere. The plaster façade was pearly white instead of gray, and the glazed windows were not yet rippled with age ... but there was no mistaking Grandmother Taemerl's house.

As they approached it, Taemerl tightened her grip on Panopael's hand, and the two of them sailed upward. Seconds later, having hurtled over the third floor balcony, they landed on the tiled floor of a rooftop garden.

Panopael stood stock still, catching her breath. Instead of Grandmother Taemerl's chaotic tangle of overgrown vines, this garden was a marvel, with flameroot trees flickering in fireproof planters and honeyfunnel blossoms drizzling nectar into brass catchpots.

Without speaking, Taemerl released Panopael's hand, crossed the patio, and disappeared into the house.

Panopael crossed her arms. "You're as rude as ever! I'm tired and I'm hungry and my face still hurts!"

When Taemerl made no reply, Panopael, feeling suddenly abandoned, crossed the patio and edged through the arched doorway. "Taemerl?"

Just inside, Taemerl, her eyes wide with wonder, sat on an ornate bed draped with embroidered fabrics. In her left hand, she held Panopael's box ... and, in her right, she held another exactly like it. She held one up. "Where did you get this?"

"I tried to tell you, but you were to busy smacking me around. You gave it to me – or you will, later."

Taemerl blinked back tears. "I

thought you had stolen the box, had been caught by the Queen Priestess, and that..."

"I was going to get away with it?"

Taemerl shook her head. "And that the Queen's death was my fault, for not keeping the box out of the wrong hands."

Panopael blinked. "Oh."

Taemerl gestured for Panopael to join her. "I gave this box to you?"

"You forced it on me. If my being here is causing trouble, it really is your fault."

Taemerl was silent for a long time. "When I was eighteen, there was talk of a new community being built across Lake Daelamr–"

"New Alfheimr?"

Taemerl nodded. "I couldn't wait to go. The day I packed my bags, my mother handed me this box and insisted I look inside. The next thing I knew, I was back here ... in the Old City ... two thousand years earlier. That was three years ago."

Panopael's eyes grew wide. "You've been trapped here for three years?"

"At the Oraculum, Queen Priestess Alva, performed a divination. She told Ellyll to take me in and treat me like a daughter – and she has."

"I can't stay here three years," Panopael said. "I've got a party tomorrow."

"Earlier, at the Oraculum, you called me 'Grandmother.' Is that right? Are you really my granddaughter?"

"When I know you, you're a lot older."

"Then I do get back home. And marry. And have children."

Panopael shrugged. "That, or at two thousand years old, you're very well preserved."

Taemerl made a face. "Apparently, in the future, I've failed to teach you proper manners."

"You've not taught me much of anything," Panopael said. "We're practically strangers."

Taemerl put her Tarot box away and returned its twin to Panopael. "It's time to change that, Panopael ... because our destinies are clearly linked."

* * * * *

Panopael followed Taemerl downstairs to the kitchen: a spartan, well-organized space with a brick oven and a charmed cabinet for chilling water, vegetables, and fruit. Taemerl produced slabs of brown bread, a pot of sweet butter, and a platter of salted ham. For the next quarter-hour, they sat at the gnarlwood table, munching sandwiches, but when a series thuds overhead announced arrivals in the rooftop garden, Taemerl quickly cleared the table and gestured for Panopael to follow her upstairs.

They found Ellyll on the second floor, in a room complete with a vaulted ceiling, leaded windows, and a small altar at one end. There, Ellyll stood in a shaft of sunlight, embracing a weeping Alberich.

Alberich could barely speak. "My mother ... and now my father?"

Ellyll patted his back. "Ssssh. We aren't sure."

Panopael wrinkled her nose and looked up at Taemerl. "A little emotional, for a prince."

Taemerl sighed. "Ellyll loves him, and she's helped him grow. At times, though, he is more child than husband."

Keeping one arm around her husband, Ellyll turned to Panopael and Taemerl. "King Oberon, Alberich's father, is missing."

Taemerl gasped. "We should summon Elders to reinforce the house's protection charm. I'll tell the Enforcers to put men with flameroot arrows on the roof –"

Before Taemerl could finish, the entire safehouse shuddered. A massive thunderclap shook the floor and rattled the windows. Alberich shrieked, covering his head with one arm and clinging to his wife with the other.

When the concussion passed, Panopael made her way to one of the chapel's tall, tapered windows. What she saw on the horizon struck terror in her heart. "There's something I think you need to see."

Chapter Four

Ellyll, Taemerl, and Alberich joined Panopael at the window. High above the city, at the crest of the Royal Ridge, the Palace was obscured by a rotating funnel of blood-red cloud.

Alberich stumbled backward. "An attack on the palace? If our attackers can penetrate palace defenses, what can we possibly do?"

Alberich's reaction frightened Panopael more than the evil-looking funnel cloud. "You're the prince! Take control!"

Alberich's pressed his hands to his head. "At any minute, the Dark Elves will strip off our skin and use it for jackets and coats!"

Panopael stamped her foot. "So get on a horse and rally the troops!"

Ellyll clapped her hands, making both Alberich and Panopael jump. "We don't have the luxury of wallowing in personal fears. Our subjects need us to survey the situation and plan a response. Taemerl, coordinate things from here.

Panopael, bring your Tarot cards. I have a feeling we'll need your help."

Ellyll's plan calmed and focused them all, but before she, Alberich, and Panopael could even reach the stairs, an out-of-breath messenger intercepted them. "Princess Ellyll ... we've found the king."

* * * * *

They arrived at the top of the Royal Ridge, where the palace courtyard was littered with fallen oaks and ever-

---

The Tarot of the Elves

greens. A few official buildings, lacking the palace's magical defenses, were reduced to rubble. The palace, though, remained intact.

Panopael scurried to keep up as Ellyll and Alberich rushed through the doors and into the entrance hall. They ran down a covered walkway, finally stopping in a sculpture garden outside a reception hall. A knot of palace attendants and Enforcers lingered here; some were weeping.

The scar-faced Enforcer Panopael recognized from earlier in the day stepped forward. "Before going in ... you should prepare yourself."

"Is my father wounded?" Alberich cried. "Is he dying?"

The Enforcer motioned for them to enter. "Perhaps both. Perhaps neither."

* * * * *

With the others, Panopael entered the receiving hall. She was shocked to see the entire roof had been peeled away. Overhead, beams as thick as Panopael's own body were snapped in half. Red-tinted sunlight filtered down in great, bloody shafts, drawing Panopael's eyes to the rear of the chamber ... and the throne.

At first, Panopael mistook the figure sitting there for a glazed statue: a bearded man with shoulder-length hair, carved from a single piece of glossy, blood red stone. His face was sober and serious; his eyes were closed as if in meditation.

Alberich gaped in disbelief. "Father?"

Ellyll lowered her eyes. "The palace's defenses were not enough, so he saved us all by absorbing the enchantment himself."

Panopael couldn't stop staring at the frozen figure. "Is he dead?"

Ellyll shook her head. "Transmuted into living stone."

Alberich touched his father's fossilized face. "Can he hear us? See us?"

"I don't think so," Ellyll said.

Panopael frowned. "If the queen is dead and the king is ... indisposed ... isn't he King Alberich?"

Ellyll nodded. "That's correct."

Alberich spun around, lost his footing, and almost fell. "What? No! I can't be king!"

"We've always known that you'd be king someday," Ellyll said.

"In name only!" Alberich ran to Ellyll, his hands pressed to his head. "Everyone knows you're the real power behind the throne!"

"I just got here," Panopael said, "and even I know it."

Ellyll dismissed all this simple gesture. "Nevertheless, you are now the King. I can help you, but if you defer constantly to my counsel, you will appear weak, and the Dark Elves will attack with even greater boldness."

Alberich staggered around the room. "We have to bring my father back!"

"There may be a way," Ellyll said, "but only divination can reveal it."

Alberich lifted his nose in the air, trying to look regal. "Then, as king, I command that the divination be performed!"

Ellyll took his hand. "If I use my powers now, I will lose our child."

Alberich pointed at Panopael. "Not by you. By her!"

The Tarot of the Elves

Chapter Five

Panopael shuffled the Tarot cards. "Is that enough?"

Ellyll shrugged. "You tell me."

"You're supposed to say, 'Shuffle the cards seven times,' or 'Chant this phrase.'"

Ellyll smiled. "Rituals have limited value, Panopael. Trust your feelings."

Panopael shuffled until the deck felt heavier, and all desire to shuffle faded away. "Ready."

"Keep things simple," Ellyll said. "Draw one card to represent the remedy needed to release King Oberon."

Panopael pulled a card from the top of the deck. On it, two Elves stood in a pool of clear water. "One's Alberich. But who's the old guy?"

"A Priest named Velorl," Ellyll said. "He's performing the Ritual of Consecration – blessing a new king."

"To fix Oberon, Alberich needs a shampoo from a priest?"

Ellyll laughed. "We must place our faith in the cards and go see Velorl."

"This reading ... it's not what I expected."

Ellyll smiled. "Divination seeks information, not affirmation."

Panopael was surprised to find herself on the verge of tears. "The kingdom hangs in the balance. Should you be listening to me?"

"To be effective, intuition must give way to action. Dry your eyes

---

and gather your cards. We have a lot to get done."

* * * * *

Surrounded by mounted Enforcers, they departed the royal stables on two horses: one for Ellyll, and one for Alberich and Panopael.

Panopael, certain the horse would rear up and toss them off any minute, locked her hands around Alberich's waist. "Why doesn't someone just magic us to see this priest?"

"Magical travel can be traced," Alberich said. "How does a girl get to be your age and not know how to ride a horse?"

"How does a Prince get to be your age and not know how to run a kingdom?"

By late afternoon, they reached a rustic temple, complete with a high-pitched wooden roof, polished stone walls, and a fruit-littered alter. The scar-faced Enforcer, cocking his head to one side, gestured for everyone to stop.

"What's wrong?" Panopael whispered.

Alberich frowned. "As we approach the Shrine of the Four Implements, the Priest should come out to greet us."

"Maybe he's busy sacrificing."

Alberich raised an eyebrow.

Panopael shrugged. "Whatever. I'm not religious."

Alberich rolled his eyes. "I've entrusted our fate to an agnostic oracle. My glorious reign begins."

Scarface dismounted, crept past the altar to the temple entrance, and ducked inside. Almost immediately, he emerged with his arm around a white-haired Elf in blood-spattered robes.

Ellyll dismounted and ran to him. "Velorl! Are these wounds serious?"

The old Elf spat. "They're serious to me. Dark Elf said he was bringing a peace offering."

Panopael eased down from Alberich's horse. "Was he swarthy? With braids on either side of his face?"

The Priest narrowed his eyes. "You're one to call people swarthy."

"This is Panopael," Ellyll said. "I trust her."

Alberich joined them, glancing at the shadowy woodlands. "This Dark Elf. Not likely still around, is he?"

Velorl shook his head. "Ran off, after ransacking the temple. Stole the Four Implements."

For the first time Panopael could recall, Ellyll's composure faltered. "What?"

Velorl shooed her away. "Don't just stand there. Run tell Oberon and Alva."

Ellyll drew three calming breaths. "Oberon has been enchanted. Alva is dead."

For once, Velorl had no reply.

"We hope to restore Oberon," Ellyll said, "but the enchantment binding him is unusually powerful. Panopael's divination suggested we'd find a remedy here."

Velorl grunted. "Then you're screwed. You need the Four Implements."

Panopael's face lit up. "Is one of your implements a silver sword?"

Velorl glared at her. "The Sword of Consciousness. It could help Oberon."

"Is one of them a cup?"

The priest arched an eyebrow. "In the hands of a priest, the Cup of Contentment could revive Queen Alva."

"How about a long metal pole?" Panopael held her hands up, as though holding an imaginary platter. "And a silver disk about this size?

Ellyll's spirits lifted. "You've seen these?"

"The Magician on the Lake Road had them," Panopael said. "He told me to tell Volundr the implements were coming."

Velorl turned pale. "If what you say is true, then everything may already be lost."

Panopael bristled. "Of course it's true."

"What Velorl means to say," Ellyll explained, "is that we are in a race against time. The Implements can be used once every thousand years. Oberon used them a millennia ago to launch the Golden Age. As of yesterday, they can be used again. The Dark Elves may be planning to use their power to launch an attack against Alfheimr."

"Worse than that," the old Elf said, his eyes brimming with tears. "Did your Magician happen to call himself The Hand of God?"

Panopael nodded.

The priest sank to his knees. "This is no Dark Elf plot."

* * * * *

Ellyll, Panopael, and Alberich joined Velorl inside the temple. The old priest spread a fragile scroll on the table and traced his finger along a line of faded runes. "Velorl lost a battle with the Sleeping God – the Maker of the Universe. As punishment, the Sleeping God bound Volundr, preventing him from taking action on his own behalf."

Velorl switched scrolls and tapped a diagram of the twelve planets. "Every twelve thousand years, an alignment gives Volundr the strength to rise from the Underworld. As a bound god, his influence is limited, but if he can persuade someone to help him..."

"... He'll break his bonds and make war again." Ellyll studied the planetary diagram. "This time, his twelve thousand year cycle overlaps the energizing of the Four Implements."

"He tricks a helper – the Hand of God – to bring him the Disc and break his bonds. Then, with the Wand of Victory, he'll slay the Sleeping God."

"Today's attacks were just distractions," Ellyll murmured.

"Or strategies," Velorl said. "The

says The Hand of God can only be stopped by the King and his seer."

"And now my father is enchanted," Alberich moaned. "And my mother is dead!"

Panopael stamped her foot. "You're the king now!"

"Enough," Ellyll said. "Officially, Alberich isn't king until he undergoes the Ritual of Consecration. Velorl, the sooner you baptize him, the better."

"Can't," Velorl said. "We use the Disc of Desire to baptize the new kings."

"Rituals have limited value," Panopael said, quoting Ellyll. "If the point is to have faith in what you're doing, couldn't you use an everyday bowl?"

Ellyll smiled. "I've never met a priest who didn't have an offering bowl."

Velorl snorted. "A spoiled boy anointed with a begging bowl. Gods help us."

* * * * *

At the crystal pool, Velorl scooped up water and poured a gentle stream over Alberich's head. "As the Priest of the Four Implements, I bestow upon you my blessing. Alberich, Son of Oberon, I greet you as my king."

From her place beside Ellyll, Panopael shivered. The babbling stream, the men in the pool, the leaves swirling in the crystal water ... every detail was exactly as she'd seen it on the Tarot card from Taemerl's box.

In that instant, the nature of the deck became clear to Panopael: the illustrations hinted at the meaning of each card, but they were also scenes from the lives of these people – legendary Elves, all but forgotten in Panopael's day. The Tarot's story was *their* story ... and now, by virtue of her immersion in it, it was her story, too.

But even with her very limited knowledge of Tarot, Panopael knew that one card was called "Death." Which of these people, she wondered, was pictured on that card?

Chapter Six

> Trump VI – The Lovers. "Alberich and Ellyll share their first night together as king and queen." *Empathy, passion, sexuality. Unions of like-minded people, or unusual coalitions coming together to work toward a common goal. The Many become The One.*

By the time they returned to Alfheimr, black banners hung on every door, announcing a period of mourning. Stores and shops were closed, but Panopael could see people inside their homes, setting tables and tending fires. A wave of homesickness swept over her, and Panopael worked hard to hold back tears.

At the safehouse, the chilly air swirled with fat flakes of snow. Panopael, shivering, dismounted. "I just spent the day with a king and queen."

"You just spent the day giving your king and queen invaluable service," Ellyll said.

My king and queen. The words stirred Panopael's emotions again, and she looked down to hide her reaction. "What now?"

Ellyll patted her shoulder. "Alberich and I need time together before the quest begins. You'll stay here, where Taemerl can see to your needs."

Panopael bid them goodnight. And then, without even thinking about it, she walked toward the wall of the safehouse, magicked herself upward through the falling snow, and landed softly on the warm stones of the roof garden.

* * * * *

Panopael, freshly bathed and

wrapped in warm robes, sat in the kitchen with Taemerl.

While Panopael had been away, Taemerl had surveyed the extent of the damage at the palace, outlined the needed repairs, and launched an army of craftsmen and magicians to carry them out. She had also worked with heralds and storytellers, crafting a concise account of the events of the day, from the murder of Queen Alva to the consecration of King Alberich.

Panopael listened to Taemerl's update, trying hard not to be distracted by the best vegetable soup she'd ever tasted. "Even back in my time, you're always working. On my best day, I don't get a fifth as much done as you do."

Taemerl, putting dishes away, laughed. "You underestimate yourself." Turning away from the cabinets, she wandered to one of the kitchen's glazed windows. Looking out, she gestured for Panopael.

Panopael reluctantly pushed back from the table, crossed to the window, and peered down. Protected by the safehouse's magic, the courtyard garden included a maze of evergreens and flowering vines, punctuated by fountains and statuary. Snow fell around the perimeter, dusting the limbs of the fir trees with winter white, but the central portion of the garden, suffused with a golden glow, was pure springtime.

It took Panopael a moment to spot Alberich and Ellyll in the middle of it all. Naked, they stood face to face, with Ellyll's pregnant belly nestled firmly against Alberich's flat stomach.

Panopael stepped back. "We shouldn't see that!"

Taemerl looked puzzled. "Two lovers embracing? It's the most natural thing in the world!"

Panopael rolled her eyes. "Don't they have rooms? Or pajamas?"

Taemerl rested her forehead against the window's chilly glass. "Don't let immaturity blind you to a rare glimpse of perfection, Panopael. Tonight, on their first night together as king and queen, Ellyll and Alberich are more than two naked people in a garden. They're a symbol of holy unity: so firmly bound together, nothing can divide them."

"People should wear clothes." Panopael crept closer to the window and looked out again. Alberich and Ellyll still embraced, gazing into each other's eyes. From out of nowhere, a sudden rush of desire welled up in Panopael – a desperate longing to find someone who could complete her in the way Ellyll completed Alberich.

When the embrace ended, Alberich and Ellyll joined hands and disappeared through the curtained doorway of the royal apartments.

Panopael turned away from the window, seated herself at the table, and pulled the box of Tarot cards from a pocket in her robe. She removed the deck, and was more amused than surprised to see the top card was The Lovers. "If I'm going to be some kind of prophet, I have to know more about what I'm doing."

Taemerl joined her. Together, they began sorting the cards, staring with the ones Panopael recognized: The Fool, The Magician, the Priestess, the Empress, the Hierophant, the Lovers. In all, there seemed to be twenty-two specially numbered cards: from card zero, The Fool, to card twenty-one, The World. Making good use of the wide kitchen table, they arranged these cards into a line.

At first, the remaining fifty-six cards struck Panopael as a bewildering jumble of random pictures. But they were also numbered, and Panopael soon realized there were four complete cycles of ten cards each: a red suit marked with a wand, a blue suit marked with a silver chalice, a yellow suit denoted by a sword, and a green suit stamped with a tiny disc.

"Are these the Four Implements?" Panopael asked.

Taemerl pointed to the four piles of color-coded cards. "Four suits, four Implements, four elements: the fiery Wand of Victory, the watery Cup of Contentment, the airy Sword of Consciousness, and the earthy Disc of Desire."

Panopael created four more lines of cards – the four suits, arranged in order from one to ten. "They tell stories!"

"The stories of the Four Implements – and how King Oberon came to own them." Taemerl tapped the line of red cards. "There's Selomir, the Dark Elf, who used the Wand of Victory to force his will on all creation. In the blue cards, you'll see Hallavae, who used the Cup of Contentment to conjure a perfect mate."

Panopael scanned the line of yellow cards. "And these?"

"Calivan was a priest who used forbidden knowledge to reanimate his murdered son ... and learned the consequences of that choice."

"And the disc story?"

"A maiden named Fadonne wanted the Disc of Desire more than anything ... but discovered that possessing something isn't always as satisfying as desiring it."

Panopael picked up the final pile of sixteen cards. "These look like portraits."

"Court cards," Taemerl said. "Or people cards: the four people who play key roles in each story."

Panopael put her head in her hands. "How does all this help with divination?"

"The suit cards tell stories about everyday people caught up in extraordinary events" Taemerl said. "Each suit explores one of life's four great pursuits: victory, love, wisdom, and satisfaction. By comparing your situation to the card, you gain unexpected insights."

Panopael fingered the first line of twenty-two cards. "These tell a story, too."

"The Major cards map the path everyone travels." She tapped four cards in sequence: The Fool, Death, The World, and, once again, the Fool. "Birth ... death ... unity with the gods ... and back again."

Panopael sniffed. "I don't believe in reincarnation."

Taemerl shrugged. "You don't have to. All you do is relate the cards to the world around you. As you become familiar with the story behind each card, you gain insights into what's happening now ... and what's most likely to happen next."

"We're living through the Majors, aren't we?"

"When I picked up the deck years ago, I was drawn into the Majors. Now the same thing has happened to you."

Panopael brightened. "So to find the Four Implements, all I have to do is look at the cards and tell Alberich what I see?"

"Possibly," Taemerl said. "Remember: the images and stories are symbolic, and have to be interpreted. That's what divination's all about."

Panopael stared down at the cards for several seconds, then gingerly pulled the thirteenth card away from the rest. "This person, face down in the water. That's Alberich, isn't it? If Alberich is going to die ... then shouldn't I stop this quest?"

Taemerl put a hand on each side of Panopael's face. "The Death card reminds us to do what we can, while we can. For you and for Alberich, that includes going on this quest, whatever the consequences."

Panopael flinched. "You mean Alberich and Ellyll. The king and his seer go on the quest."

Taemerl blinked. "No one explained this to you?"

"Explained what?"

Taemerl lowered her voice. "Ellyll is pregnant, and cannot use her powers. In her absence, Panopael ... you're the seer."

Chapter Seven

The morning sky was low and gray, packed with clouds and punctuated by occasional peals of thunder. Overnight, outside the eternal springtime of the safehouse, bitter cold had blackened young plants and dusted the ground with hard frost. A brutal north wind ripped through the streets of Alfheimr, ripping the black mourning banners to shreds.

Panopael hadn't slept. No protest, no objection, no tearful appeal – not even the genuine tearful appeal that had burst out, raw and unexpected, after Panopael had delivered a very convincing fake one – would free her from her obligation to accompany Alberich on his quest. Taemerl had been polite, but firm; Elven law was Elven law.

Now, wrapped in Taemerl's warmest fur-lined coat, Panopael stood with a dozen other Elves at the city's Eastern Gate. She was staring at the frozen ground, lost in thought, when the scar-faced Enforcer approached her.

"Last night, we received word that someone matching the description of your Magician – a Dark Elf named Dokkalfar – was seen in a town near the Western Ridge. He's bragging that he's waiting for you."

Panopael didn't look up. "Thanks for that."

"Meantime, there's word of something strange going on near the volcanic park. Something ... unnatural. You might start your quest there." Scarface paused, waiting for Panopael's reply. When none came, he added, "But I guess your little cards have already told you everything you need to know."

Panopael glared at him. "What's your problem?"

The man snorted and spat on the ground. "A king should have a fighter by his side – not a dreamer." With that, he turned and walked away.

* * * * *

Ellyll and Alberich arrived, bundled in winter cloaks and walking hand in hand; almost immediately, Ellyll motioned for Panopael to join them.

"You're taking my place on a very difficult journey, Panopael. I wanted you to thank you for that ... and for all you're doing for the Elves of Alfheimr."

"Sure."

Ellyll winked, then pulled a velvet pouch from her pocket. From it, she removed a silver chain with a single pendant attached. As she placed the chain around Alberich's neck, the pendant flared to life, giving off a blue-white glow. "When you're close to me, the pendant is brilliant; when you're far away, it dims. When we're reunited, it will burn as brightly as a sun."

With that, Ellyll kissed Alberich on the lips. "Alberich, you be the king I know you to be." Next, she took Panopael's hand and placed it on her pregnant belly. "Panopael, you bring my husband home."

Panopael's breath came in short hitches. She felt like a trapped animal; she wanted to cry out, to tell Ellyll that she would very likely never see Alberich again. In the end, though, all she could do was nod; had she spoken aloud, she would have collapsed in sobs.

As if on cue, guards brought around the royal chariot: an elaborate vehicle, constructed of a single piece of bright steel. Pulled by two horses – one black, the other white – it was stabilized by powerful magic; as Panopael and Alberich climbed in, the chariot didn't wobble in the least.

Alberich, sensing the gravity of the moment, cleared this throat. "I stand here today on the verge of an all-important quest." His voice cracked, making him sound almost as frightened and uncertain as Panopael l felt. "I go to retrieve the Four Implements and restore the kingdom. As is the custom, I take no weapons with me; instead, I carry a wise advisor and..." He trailed off, as though at a loss for words. "And that's it, I guess."

Ellyll smiled. "It's time, Panopael. Picture where you want to go, and the chariot will take you there."

Panopael closed her eyes, forcing twin tears to roll down both sides of her face. In her head, she pictured

The Tarot of the Elves

the image from the Strength card: Alberich wrestling a mechanical monster in the midst of a volcanic landscape.

The metal body of the chariot began to vibrate, then hum. A ghostly glow spread over the skin of the vehicle; almost immediately, the horses lurched forward.

As the chariot pulled away, Panopael kept her eyes on the amulet around Alberich's neck. Its light held steady at first; finally, though, it flickered, dimmed, and faded entirely.

* * * * *

The chariot glided effortlessly over rough terrain; apparently, the charm animating it also insulated the occupants from fatigue. As a result, apart from one or two necessary stops, Panopael and Alberich made surprising progress. As the landscape changed from the grassy plains of the Alfheimr Valley to the increasingly rocky foothills of the Western Ridge, the pair maintained a peculiar, but not uncomfortable, silence.

Eventually, late in the afternoon, Alberich cleared his throat and spoke. "We'll be coming to the western border soon."

Panopael shrugged. "Okay."

"After that, the road won't be so good, and the terrain gets trickier."

"Trickier?"

Alberich sniffed. "Trickier as in volcanoes and sulfur pools and ther-mal vents and gas clouds. Trickier as in the edge of Dark Elf territory."

Panopael sighed. "You're such a big chicken."

The tips of Alberich's ears turned bright red. "I'm just wondering if your divination revealed any options beyond walking straight into the lion's mouth."

"You have a better idea?"

"You're my advisor!"

Panopael rolled her eyes. "If you didn't have a woman telling you what to do, you couldn't put your pants on in the mornings."

"You will not address the king that way!"

"I can't address the king that way. Ellyll's not here!"

Alberich stood and stamped his foot. "Treason!"

"Truth!"

Even as they warmed to the argument, the chariot lurched to a sudden stop.

"Why aren't we moving?" Panopael asked.

Alberich gulped. "We're at Kingdom's Edge."

The road ahead led through an ornate stone arch, flanked by scattered boulders – the remains of an ancient wall. Further on, the land shimmered with a dull red illumination. The warm air reeked of sulfur.

Panopael recalled Scarface's warning: *Something strange going on near the volcanic park. Something ... unnatural.* She shivered. "I can't say I blame the horses for stopping."

Alberich, nibbling his lower lip, scanned their surroundings. Suddenly, he pointed to the archway. "There. You see?"

Panopael shielded her eyes with her hands. Atop the archway sat an elaborate metal figure: a tiny dragon, smaller than a horse, with gleaming silver scales and white crystal eyes. "That's just a statue, Alberich."

"Of course it's a statue," Alberich snapped. "But it looks ... out of place."

Recalling the image from the Strength card, Panopael brightened. "Scarface said Dokkalfar's been seen in the nearby city. Maybe, before going into town, he hid one of the implements inside that thing."

Alberich nodded. "Go check it out."

"You can't be serious."

Alberich made a face. "Are you here to serve the king or not?"

"Aww," Panopael purred. "Is the wittle bitty dwagonette gonna get the gweat big king of the –"

From the corner of her eye, Panopael saw the flicker of sunlight on bright metal. One of the horses *screamed* – the most human sound Panopael had ever heard from an animal – and an instant later, the chariot, Panopael, and Alberich went tumbling through the air.

The Tarot of the Elves

Chapter Eight

> *Trump VIII – Strength.*
> "Alberich wrestles the Dragonette." *Strength, power, force. Willpower and triumph over temptation. Brute force, raw physical effort, or specialized training. Achieving more by bringing one's efforts and skills into alignment with Divine Will.*

Panopael, dazed, struggled to stand.

The chariot, no longer glowing, lay upside down on the side of the road. Alberich, unmoving, lay face down in the grass. The black horse ran around them in crazy circles, snorting. The white horse was gone.

"Alberich!"

In lieu of a reply, Panopael heard a distant whistling noise. Faint at first, it rapidly increased in volume: the sound of something large and solid flying through the air in her direction. By instinct, she dropped to the ground. Something streaked overhead. An instant later, she heard the sound of a blunt impact ... and a terrified animal's scream.

In the silence that followed, Panopael realized she could no longer hear the hoof beats of the panicked black horse. When she looked up, he was nowhere to be seen.

Panopael, expecting another attack at any moment, scrambled to her feet and ran to Alberich's side. Panopael scrambled to her feet. "Get up! We have to move!"

Alberich regained consciousness with a jolt. He jerked to his knees, flailed his arms, and fell backward, almost knocking Panopael over in the process. "Retreat!" he shouted. "Retreat!"

"Retreat to where?" Panopael yelled.

Somewhere above them, high in the sky, Panopael heard the whistling sound begin. Glancing up, she saw its source: a gleaming pinpoint of light, growing larger by the second.

Alberich blinked. "I was right!"

"About what?"

"About the dragonette! For once, I listened to my instincts, scented the air, and looked for clues –"

Panopael grabbed Alberich by the arm and, putting all her strength into it, yanked him to a standing position. "We ... have ... got ... to ... move!"

With Alberich in tow, Panopael ran toward the chariot. She didn't know if its magic would allow it to travel without the horses, but, if nothing else, its metal shell might offer some protection from the dragonette's attacks.

An instant later, the air filled with a terrible metallic shriek. The dragonette rammed into the ground just behind Panopael and Alberich. Chunks of earth streamed into the air. The concussion following the impact knocked both Elves to the ground.

Panopael glanced back. Behind them, the dragonette emerged from a steaming crater. The beast appeared to be made of rippling, living metal, with a sinuous tail that screeched like a rusty door hinge. Its crystal eyes were as bright as the seebeams on the front of a water carriage, and its gaping jaws were lined with sharp chrome teeth.

Keeping low, the dragonette dug its sharp talons into the earth and roared at them.

And then, Panopael saw it: the creature's tongue was also metal – long, sharp, shiny ... and instantly familiar. "The Sword of Consciousness," Panopael said. "It's got the Sword of Consciousness for a tongue. Dokkalfar used the Sword of Consciousness to bring it to life!"

Alberich shook his head. "That can't be right. If he did, then the sword can't be used for another thousand years ... and a lot of people wouldn't be happy about that, including You Know Who."

"What are you saying?"

"Dark Elves are master mechanics," Alberich said. "The dragonette's probably just an elaborate machine with the Sword hidden inside until your Magician friend needs it."

"So what do we do next?"

"We could ask it very nicely to hand over the sword..."

The dragonette tensed its muscles, preparing to pounce.

Alberich shrugged. "Or we could run."

They ran, and, desperate for cover, dove behind the upended chariot.

Seconds later, the dragonette charged. There was a terrible sound of metal on metal, as though the world's largest blacksmith had pounded the world's largest sword with the world's largest hammer – and then, nothing.

Until Panopael opened her eyes, she hadn't realized she'd clamped them shut. Beside her, Alberich crouched down, hands over his head, whimpering.

Panopael peeked over the rim of the chariot. She expected to come face to face with the flashing jaws of the dragonette; instead, about halfway to the horizon, she saw the beast strike the ground, raising another explosive cloud of rocks and earth.

"It bounced," Panopael said.

"The chariot's stabilizing magic! Even with the chariot upside down, it deflected the blow!" Alberich almost stood up, but thought the better of it. "Is that thing still coming for us?"

Panopael held her breath. In the distance, the impact cloud was still settling. Seconds ticked slowly by. A minute. Two.

And then, screaming with fury, the dragonette emerged from the lip of the new crater.

"It's coming again," Panopael said. "I don't know what to do."

"Pull out your cards!"

"Now? In the middle of a crisis?"

"What better time?"

Panopael dug the box from the folds of her cloak, removed the cards, and shuffled them. As she did so, the Chariot card popped out. "Ooops."

Alberich rolled his eyes. "Stick it in and shuffle again!"

Panopael retrieved the card and resumed shuffling. This time, the Chariot card seemed to jump from the deck of its own accord, falling to the ground face up.

In the distance, the dragonette streaked up into the sky.

"How can you read cards that you can't even shuffle?"

Panopael scooped up the Chariot card, stuffed it into the deck, and shuffled like mad. "Tell me how we can defeat the dragonette," she whispered. She drew a single card: the Chariot.

Alberich held out his hand. "Give me those cards!"

"No!" Panopael snatched the deck away, shielding them with her body. "Don't you see? The same card is jumping out again and again." She paused, squeezing her forehead with one hand. "The Chariot! Of course!"

High overhead, the whistle of the dragonette's approach began.

"Clock's ticking," Alberich said.

"When I wanted the chariot to take us somewhere, all I did was picture it in my mind." Panopael put the cards away, drew a deep breath, and closed her eyes.

Abruptly, the chariot righted itself.

"What now?" Alberich asked.

"I pictured you pulling the sword from the dragonette's mouth – and the chariot responded." Panopael glanced up; the dragonette was plummeting directly down toward them. "Quick – get in!"

Alberich obeyed. "And now?"

Panopael started to reply – but before she could, the chariot streaked up into the sky. Alberich, his hair flapping and his lips frozen in a round "O" of horror, went with it. Seconds later, the dragonette and the chariot collided.

Chapter Nine

> **Trump IX – The Hermit.**
> "Alberich retrieves the elven disc." *Isolation, withdrawal, retreat. Revising plans and consulting experts. Pausing to regroup. Seeking wisdom from within. Believing, correctly or incorrectly, that no outside help or aid is needed. Being a loner.*

First came the flash. Next came the sound of collision: a shriek of metal on metal, loud enough to make Panopael cover her ears.

The dragonette, its sliver limbs dangling, crashed to the earth. Shortly afterward, dozens of silver gears and clockwork springs showered down, littering the ground at Panopael's feet. An instant later, the chariot swooped in for a landing.

Alberich, clutching the sides of the vehicle, leaned over the side and vomited.

Panopael kept her distance. "Are you ... ?"

Alberich retched again, then drew a ragged breath. "I'm fine."

"Is it ... ?"

Alberich wiped his mouth on his sleeve. "Has to be."

"Do you have ... ?"

Alberich, still unsteady, hefted the Sword of Consciousness aloft.

Panopael ran to Alberich and hugged him. Alberich, tears streaming down his face, merely stared at his own reflection in the sword's gleaming blade.

* * * * *

Alberich was none the worse for wear ... but the chariot had not fared so well. Deep gashes as wide as Panopael's hands marred the side of the vehicle. No matter how hard Panopael concentrated, the chariot would not respond again. Abandoning it on the roadside felt ungrateful, but, in the end, they had no choice; night was falling, and it was time to move on.

They trudged across a vast plain of sharp, hardened lava, dodging steam vents and avoiding bubbling pools. Eventually, they wound up on a gravel path through the snow-covered foothills of the Western Range. In the distance, Panopael spotted a pair of twin mountains; Alberich called them the Ancestors – the first mountains the gods ever created.

When they reached a stone shelf on the side of a steep hill, Alberich suggested that they should stop and make camp; Panopael barely nodded before plopping down on the ground.

Alberich, humming to himself, chanted a firesong, pulled food from his pack, and warmed their dinner. The spicy scent of cooking meat brought Panopael out of her half-sleep, and she joined Alberich by the fire. "You're in a good mood."

Alberich thumped his chest. "King Alberich single-handedly slew a dragon today."

Panopael arched an eyebrow. "You weren't exactly single-handed. And, strictly speaking, it was just a dragonette."

"I also recovered an Implement today. It was easy, once I put my mind to it."

Panopael laughed. "You mean once *I* put *my* mind to it. I'm the one who sent the chariot crashing into the thing."

"And I'm the one who pulled out the sword. Admit it. I was kingly."

Panopael considered this. "When you held up the sword – after the vomiting – you did look kind of kingly."

Alberich goosed her. "Kind of?"

Panopael pulled away. "Okay! You were totally kingly."

Alberich held his chin high. "Don't forget it. Now, my seer ... consult your cards. What's next?"

"I already know," Panopael said. "The next card is called the Hermit."

"What does it show?"

"You. In a place like this. Finding the Disc of Desire on a rocky shelf."

Alberich froze. "Like on that rocky shelf right over there?"

* * * * *

Panopael couldn't believe her eyes. While she hadn't known quite what to expect, she would never have imagined that they would find the Disc of Desire just lying out in plain view. "Why would the Magician just drop it here?"

"Because he heard Alberich the Dragonslayer was closing in."

Panopael shook her head. "This doesn't make sense."

Alberich spat in disgust. "You know what this is really about? This is about King Alberich finding the Disc of Desire all on his own, without any divinatory assistance from Priestess Panopael."

"What?"

"Admit it. I spotted it. You can't stand not getting credit." Alberich reached for the disc.

"Wait!" Panopael fished in her cloak. "Let's at least do a reading on it."

Alberich rolled his eyes. "Fine. Shuffle your cards. Feel useful."

Fuming, Panopael shuffled the deck and drew a single card – The Wheel – but it came out of the deck upside-down. "I don't think this is good."

Alberich peered down. "It's trump number ten. Doesn't that one come right after trump number nine, the Hermit?"

"Yes, but–"

"So we're finished with the Hermit, and now the deck's telling us to move on." Again, Alberich reached for the disc.

Panopael planted herself between Alberich and the Implement. "Listen to me. This card's not like the others. It's reversed – upside down."

Alberich took the card from Panopael, turned it right side up, and returned it. "Happy?"

"It's not that simple. Taemerl told me a reversed card could mean a blockage of some kind – interference or obstacles."

"And here you are, standing between me and the disc!"

"There's more. Since the Wheel can mean luck or fate, the *reversed* Wheel suggests this disc might not be here by accident. It might have been left here deliberately ... as a trap."

"Step aside."

"Panopael, as your king, I order you to step aside."

Panopael pressed her lips together until they were white ... but finally she put her cards away and stepped back.

Alberich wasted no time, stepping forward and snatching up the disc. "See? No trap. Two down, one to go."

Panopael peered down at the natural shelf. There, a tiny silver disc – only a fraction of the size of the Disc of Desire – floated just above the rock, spinning slowly, but picking up speed. "What's that?"

"Another disc?" Alberich cocked his head to one side. "And it's singing."

Panopael shushed him. As the disc spun faster, the sound it made became clearer and clearer: a man's voice, chanting the same phrase over and over again. "Where have I heard that before?"

Alberich sniffed the air. "And what have you been eating? That smells like a chest poultice mixed with rotten eggs!"

Panopael's eyes widened. "Camphor and sulfur! Alberich, it's a –"

Panopael felt an all-too-familiar surge of heat and pressure ... and then, an instant later, she felt nothing at all.

Chapter Ten

Trump X – The Wheel. "The Elsirins' whirling dance seals Alberich's fate." *Cycles, circularity, fate. The machinery of Destiny revealed. Patterns and repetitions. The changing of the seasons, the turning of the tide. A life-changing moment on which much depends.*

Panopael opened her eyes.

Moments earlier, she had been tumbling through an inky blackness that seemed to go on forever. At first, Alberich had been with her; eventually, though, he had been ripped away, his screams blotted out by the roar of the icy wind.

Now, she was lying in a meadow; Alberich, face down in the grass, lay beside her. Overhead, dark, bloated clouds, criss-crossed with bolts of yellow lightning, drifted through a blood-red sky. The only other thing in her field of vision was a massive stone tower so tall it seemed on the verge of puncturing the heavens.

Still dizzy, she sat up slowly; when her eyes focused, she almost passed out again. Smiling down at her, his eyes as wild and strange as ever, was the Magician. He stood with his back to the base of the tower, flanked by four identical Elven maidens. Each had flowers woven into her long, blonde hair; each

wore dresses fashioned from thin white gossamer.

Each carried one of the Four Implements.

The Magician grinned, showing teeth. "Some would argue that Fate brought you here – that you were carried to this place and time, like leaves on the surface of a fast-flowing river by the single-minded machinery of Destiny. Is that what you believe, Panopael?"

Alberich moaned, rolling over and opening his eyes.

"Others would say you came here of your own free will – that Destiny supplies the pattern, but that your choices shape your individual fate. Tell me, Panopael, seer of the King Alberich: which version of the story do you prefer?"

Alberich sat up, took in the sky, the tower, the attendants, and the leering Magician. "This is bad, isn't it?"

"I took a risk, of course, leaving you a trail of Implements," the Magician said. "But unlike the Elves who outwardly cheered and inwardly wept as you headed out, I believed in you both. And now, as I expected, the Four Implements are reunited. Soon, I will pass them to my benefactor, and then we'll see who winds up being king of the Elves."

Alberich stood. "I've come for the Four Implements ... and to return you to Alfheimr to stand trial for the murder of King Oberon and Queen Priestess Alva – my parents."

The Magician smiled. "How many times has the cycle of failure played out in the course of your lifetime, Alberich? You want something ... getting it proves difficult ... and so you change course. Why should today be any different?"

"I'm not the person I was," Alberich said.

"That can be tested." The Magician made a gesture; a stone table appeared. The four attendants moved forward and placed the Four Implements on its surface. "One of these implements is real; the other three are false. A true king can see the difference. Choose the authentic implement, Alberich, and you may use its power to strike me down and return

home. But if you fail, my Master will deliver a punishment far greater than you can possibly imagine."

Panopael took Alberich's hand. "Don't do it."

"I need the Sword to save my father," Alberich said. "And the Cup to save my mother. Even if those were the authentic implements, I couldn't use them to defeat you without sacrificing one of my parents."

The Magician bowed. "As a king, surely you understand that all choices have consequences."

Panopael tugged at Alberich's sleeve. "This game has to be a trick. The only way to win is not to play."

The Magician giggled. "If it weren't for having a woman to tell you what to do, you probably couldn't put you pants on in the morning."

Panopael blushed. "I didn't mean that when I said it."

The Magician brushed her comment away. "I thought one of your more astute insights, really. Meantime, the answer here is glaringly obvious. You're either up to the challenge, Alberich, or you're not. Be the king. Make a choice."

Without hesitation, Alberich walked forward and took hold of the Sword of Consciousness. "I choose this one."

"Why?"

"Because you wouldn't risk everything by putting one of the real Implements on the table. And this one, real or not, is a fine weapon." That said, Alberich gripped the sword and, with all his remaining strength, swung it at the Magician.

The Tarot of the Elves

Chapter Eleven

> *Trump XI – Justice.* "Alberich loses a trial by combat." *Rules and regulations, trials and tests. Balance, logic, and objectivity. Equality or equalization; the restoration of power or retribution for its abuse. Administration of punishment. Difficult decisions made with finesse.*

The sword struck the Magician squarely in the jaw; had it been real, Alberich's blow would have taken the top of the Dark Elf's head off. Instead, the weapon popped like a soap bubble and vanished.

Alberich, overbalanced, pitched forward. He struck the side of his head on the stone table, went limp, and fell to the ground. Panopael ran to his side and shook him, but he was out cold.

Panopael glared up at the Magician. "You lied."

The Magician shrugged this off. "And you could have saved him, if you've been doing your job. Look at the tabletop, Priestess Panopael."

Panopael peered at the remaining objects. Too late, she noticed the tell-tale shimmer that blurred the edges of every single one.

The Magician glanced up at the darkening sky. "The only test here, Panopael, was really for you ... and you've failed it

completely. Because of you, Alberich will die, and the Four Implements will free Volundr from the chains imposed by the Sleeping God."

Panopael tried to speak, but words failed her.

The Dark Elf continued: "But for now, if I am to receive my reward and become king of all Elves, there are forms to be observed ... and Elven law dictates that kingship may be passed on by blood alone – if not passed on by family ties, then by the spilling of it."

Panopael shook her head. "This isn't fair."

The Dark Elf smiled. "This is not about fairness; it's about law." He turned to the four pale, identical women. "I will finish him in a trial by combat. Take him."

The woman encircled Alberich and Panopael. To Panopael's surprise, they began dancing in a slow circle. As the dance continued, they moved faster and faster, eventually moving so quickly Panopael became convinced they had grown in number.

Eventually, their bodies blurred and rippled, and all illusion of beauty and frailty faded away. The creatures were now hairless hunched figures with skin the color of eggplants. As the dance continued, leathery wings unfolded from between their protruding shoulder blades and jagged claws sprouted from their hands and feet.

Panopael had read about such creatures once, years ago: *Elsirin*. In folk tales, they appeared as beautiful maidens, calling in the middle of the night, seeking shelter. If turned away, they transformed into bat-like minions of Erlkonig – Death himself – and bore their inhospitable prey away to seek shelter in the Underworld.

In one swift move, the Elsirin dug their claws into the fabric of Alberich's tunic and cloak, plucked him out of Panopael's arms, and, with a great beating of wings, carried him into the air.

"No!" Panopael jumped, trying to grab the hem of Alberich's cloak. Her hands slipped away, and the Elsirin carried Alberich to the pinnacle of the tower.

The Dark Elf chuckled. "And another failure. But don't worry, Panopael – your shattered soul won't have long to ache."

With that, Dokkalfar, too, streaked up into the sky, ascending directly to the tower's summit.

* * * * *

Panopael dropped heavily to the ground. "It's over," she whispered. "We failed."

There was nothing to do now except wait for Alberich's death and the Elsirins' return. It was too much to bear. Panopael burst into tears, weeping with such force that she could no longer sit upright. Racked with sobs, she fell forward ... and dislodged the box of Tarot cards from her cloak in the process.

Panopael wiped her eyes and stared down at the box. Could a reading help in a situation this dire?

Too weary and defeated to come up with a question, she half-heartedly opened the box, shuffled the cards, and whispered, "Please ... help me."

She drew The Magician.

Seeing the Dark Elf's grinning face made her furious. She jammed the card back in the deck, shuffled ... and drew the same card once again.

"I know what my *problem* is! I need a *solution!*" She slapped the card back into the deck and shuffled furiously; before she could draw, a single card jumped out of the deck and landed face-up on the ground before her.

The Magician.

She was on the verge of tears again. "I don't understand! Why keep giving me The Magician?" She shook her head. "I'm sick to death of magicians ... and tricks ... and magic!"

Magic. She hesitated. "Is that it? Should I be using magic in some way?" She shuffled the cards, drew one, and, once again, received The Magician.

"Okay, magic. But I don't have any spells or implements with me. I've run out of magic."

Even as she spoke those words aloud, a memory popped into her head: a conversation with Taemerl that felt as though it had taken place years ago, even though she'd been in her grandmother's house just days before.

Panopael had been sitting in her grandmother's parlor, looking down at the Tarot cards. The old woman had come plodding down the stairs, and Panopael, angry and irritated, had said, "Run out of magic?"

"Run out of magic?" Taemerl had replied. "Elves are magic. You've just forgotten it."

Panopael shivered. "But what can I do?" She looked down at the card in her hand. *Magic.*

From out of nowhere came another memory: Taemerl popping from place to place to in the wink of an eye.

Suddenly inspired, Panopael scrambled through the Tarot deck, desperately searching for the Justice card. When she found it, she studied the picture – Alberich and the Dark Elf fighting atop the tower. As best she could, she memorized the image, then put it away with the rest of the cards.

Panopael stood, took a deep breath, and peered up into the sky. "Who needs a chariot?" she murmured ... and then, with the image of the tower's top pictured clearly in her mind, she simply disappeared.

* * * * *

A heartbeat later, Panopael found herself at the top of the tower. She felt a rush of exhilaration – *I did it!* – but it was quickly squelched.

The tower's pinnacle was nothing more than a compact circular arena, perhaps twenty paces wide, surrounded by a low lip of wall. Alberich lay on the far edge of the space, bruised and beaten. Three of the Four Implements – the Cup, the Sword, and the Disc – lay scattered on the rough stones ... and Dokkalfar, the Wand of Victory held over his head, was closing in for the kill.

"The forms have been observed," Dokkalfar shouted, straining to be heard over the sound of the raw, icy wind. "You have been tested in a trial by combat, and your loss confirms your unworthiness!"

Alberich, sensing the end, rose to his knees. "I am Alberich, Son of Oberon, the rightful King of Alfheimr. This battle was a sham, and your claim to the kingdom is not legitimate. In the eyes of Elven law, you're nothing more than a thug."

The Dark Elf gripped the wand at one end, preparing to swing it like a club. "Alberich, King of Alfheimr ... prepare to meet my God."

Chapter Twelve

> *Trump XII – The Hanged Man.* "Alberich tumbles from a great height, the four Implements falling with him." *Inversion, reversals, unwanted insight. Transformation through trial, punishment, or labor. Difficulty as a path to enlightenment. Unexpected betrayals.*

Panopael, as yet unseen, lifted her hand, extended it toward the Magician, and, with all her might, focused on a single word: *No!*

For Panopael, time slowed down. Deep within her chest, her heart gave a thunderous beat. The force of it sent a tremor down her arm, through her hand, and into her fingertips. From there, the tremor streamed outward, creating ripples in the icy air: pure magical energy.

The wave crossed the arena in an instant, striking the Dark Elf squarely between the shoulders. The Magician fell backward; the Wand of Victory clattered to the floor. The Dark Elf clawed at the low stone lip around the tower's perimeter, but it was no use; before he could regain his balance, he sailed off the edge and cartwheeled out into the open air.

Panopael literally jumped for joy ... but this personal victory, too, was fleeting. The wave of magical force continued across the arena, crackling with enough energy to Panopael's hair stand on end. As she watched in horror, it dragged the Four Implements along in its wake, then swept them, along with Alberich, over the lip of the tower.

* * * * *

Panopael screamed and ran across the arena. Her head was as clear as it had ever been, and her

The Tarot of the Elves

heart was firmly in command of every step she took.

Determined to save Alberich, she launched herself into the air.

* * * * *

Panopael fell.

Fighting against the roar of the wind, she struggled to regain some sense of balance or perspective. In the distance, she heard the clanging of the Four Implements as they tumbled through space. She thought she caught a glimpse of Alberich, his long hair rippling above him like a golden flame.

But all too soon, the world was reduced to a tumbling, featureless blur. Without the ability to focus her newfound powers, she was helpless. Everything was in the hands of gravity now.

Panic gave way to regret; regret gave way to a pang of loss. When these passed, Panopael was surprised to discover she felt perfectly calm.

I tried, she thought. *I really tried.*

Panopael gave herself over to the fall.

Chapter Thirteen

> **Trump XIII – Death.** "Erlkonig, the elven God of Death, celebrates the death of Alberich." *Conclusion, transition, transformation. The end of one phase of existence and the passage to another. Awareness of one's own mortality or a desire to live life more fully.*

The impact Panopael expected never came.

Instead, she found herself standing on a vast, blackened plain beneath a gray and featureless sky. Gingerly, as though she were afraid the motion would disrupt the landscape, she turned around ... and spotted Alberich standing further up the hill.

Panopael ran to him and, surprising even herself, embraced him. "I thought I'd lost you."

After a moment, Alberich returned her embrace. "The last thing I remember, the Magician was about to crack my head open with the Wand of Victory." He took Panopael by the shoulders and held her at arm's length. "Did you stop him?"

Before Panopael could reply, someone else answered for her: "She did indeed!"

Alberich and Panopael whirled. Behind them, her hair in golden braids and her white robes gleaming, stood Queen Priestess Alva.

* * * * *

For a long time, neither Alberich nor Panopael could do more than gape. When Alva held out her hands, the spell was shattered, and Alberich ran to his mother.

"How is it possible?" Alberich cried. "You're alive!"

Alva patted him on the back. "Guess again."

Alberich's grin faded. "We're ... dead?"

Alva laughed. "Nothing ever dies. Besides ... does this look like the realm of the dead to you?"

Panopael took in the colorless sky and the ruined landscape. "It's not what I'd call a celebration of life."

Alva stepped away from her son and approached Panopael. "Speaking of celebrations: I have much to thank you for."

"I don't see why," Panopael said. "We weren't exactly successful."

"That depends on how you measure success," Alva said. "In his darkest hour, did my son respond with bravery?"

"He did," Panopael admitted.

"And in your darkest hour ... were you willing to give yourself completely to save someone else?"

Panopael blinked, surprised at herself. "I was."

"Irresponsible Alberich, responding with bravery. Selfish Panopael, sacrificing herself for someone else. That sounds like success."

Alberich frowned. "But then we died – or something – didn't we?"

Alva smiled. "Or something." She gestured at the landscape around them. "We're *between*. Bliss above, darkness below. Having been caught up in a struggle larger than ourselves, we're suspended until the final outcome is known."

Alberich considered this.

"Where's this Magician? I'd like to move him a little farther from bliss and a little closer to darkness."

Alva shook her head. "Dokkalfar took flight; he did not fall."

Panopael fished around in her cloak and produced her Tarot cards. "It's not that I'm unhappy to see you ... but I don't think that any of this is what was supposed to happen."

Alva arched an eyebrow. "Oh?"

Panopael removed the Tarot deck and thumbed through the cards until she found Trump XIII. "The card shows Alberich face down in the water and someone ... or something ... looming over him, with the Wand of Victory held in the air."

"Do you notice anything unusual about that card?"

Panopael studied it. "It scares me more than the others."

Alva laughed. "Compare it to the others in the deck."

Panopael pulled several cards, comparing them to the Death trump. "Every other card looks realistic: detailed backgrounds, realistic objects. By comparison, the Death card looks ... fake."

"Because they're drawn by the living, images of Death reflect our fears of death, but never the realities. Barring death by violence, we Elves are virtually immortal, so our Death card shows Erlkonig, our god of death, claiming us the only way he can – in battle."

Panopael gave the landscape a nervous glance. "Is this Erlkonig character around here somewhere?"

"He's a legend, Panopael ... a way to picture death, but not truly a part of it." Alva smiled. "There's one other card in your deck that looks vague and unrealistic. When you see it later on, remember: there's a reason for that."

Alberich, suddenly frantic, scrambled around, scanning the landscape. "Wait a minute ... where are the Four Implements?"

"Being of the world, they remain in it."

Alberich pointed to Panopael. "She gets her Tarot cards!"

"That should tell you something about Tarot," Alva said, her eyes twinkling.

Panopael looked down at her Tarot deck with renewed respect, then, very carefully put the cards away. "So the Four Implements – they're still in the hands of The Magician?"

Alva nodded. "And even now, Dokkalfar plans to give them to Volundr."

"Can we do anything about that from here?" Panopael asked.

"If you're willing to make certain sacrifices," Alva said, "you can do a great deal."

Chapter Fourteen

> *Trump XIV – Temperance.*
> "Medelvae, the elven goddess of healing and medicine, eases Alberich's passage back to the Overworld." *Healing, meditation, rejuvenation. Restoring lost balance by avoiding extremes. Making amends or repenting for past wrongs. Accepting consequences with grace.*

Alva, Alberich, and Panopael set out across the blackened landscape, following a well-worn path through a featureless valley. Gradually, the sky brightened, and grass and wildflowers broke through the hard-baked earth. The first trees they encountered were stunted and twisted, but soon, these gave way to towering oaks, pomegranate shrubs, and lush greenery.

"We are going to see Medelvae," Alva explained. "She's the Mediator, charged with maintaining the balance of power between light and darkness. Souls may linger here, between worlds, for only a short time; eventually, everyone must visit Medelvae, who sends them on to bliss ... or blight."

"Bliss sounds good," Panopael said.

"But how does our moving on to bliss or darkness help the situation back home?" Alberich asked.

They came to an ornate gateway – the boundary of a tropical garden. Overhead, rainbow-hued birds played in the heavily laden branches of the fruit trees; beneath their feet, a mist rose from the earth, drenching the ferns and grasses with dew.

Alva opened the gate for them, but did not go inside. "I believe your coming here upsets the balance of events in the Overworld. When that's the case, Medelvae has license to offer souls other choices ... for a price. But remember: Medelvae is a goddess; her ways are not our ways. Keep that in mind, when striking bargains."

Alberich straightened his shoulders. "Whatever the price, I'll find a way to pay it."

"I have faith in you. I always have." Alva gestured to the garden. "You should go."

Alberich hesitated. "You're not going with us?

"Souls who go to see Medelvae are ready to have their fate decided." Alva sighed deeply. "I'm not ready yet."

Alberich hugged his mother close. "I can't lose you again!"

Alva patted his back and stroked his hair. "You never lost me to begin with, Alberich; the world offered you a dream of separation, and you dreamed that dream for a time. That's all."

* * * * *

In the middle of the garden, they came to a crystal pool. Beside it, a longhaired maiden with blindingly white robes sat cross-legged on the ground, deep in meditation.

Panopael cleared her throat. If the maiden heard anything, she didn't respond.

"So do we wait?" Panopael asked.

Alberich approached the placid woman and extended a hand. "I'm done waiting."

Before Alberich could touch her,

Medelvae's eyes snapped open. In a flash, she locked her hand around his wrist. "You are Alberich, son of King Oberon, son of Queen Priestess Alva. You are a coward, and you are brave. You are a husband and father, a boy and a king."

Alberich tried to pull away. "That hurts!"

The maiden refused to let go; instead, she offered Panopael her other hand. Reluctantly, Panopael took it.

Medelvae's grip was fierce; Panopael felt the small bones in her hand shift under the pressure. "You are Panopael, daughter of Filhardil, daughter of Janilr. You are selfish, and you are selfless. You are daughter and granddaughter, a girl ... and a Priestess."

"You're getting a bit ahead of yourself," Panopael said. "I'm not a Priestess."

Medelvae released them both, then closed her eyes again. A chill breeze swept into the garden, whipping the mist behind Medelvae into a gauzy spiral shot through with shafts of golden sunlight. In the center of the swirling mist, an image took shape: Alberich standing in the chapel of the safehouse.

From somewhere in the mist, they heard Panopael's voice: "If the queen is dead and the king is indisposed, isn't he King Alberich?"

The image of Alberich spun around, lost its footing, and pinwheeled its arms. "What? No! I can't be king!"

The Tarot of the Elves

Then came Ellyll's voice, gentle and low: "We've always known you'd be king someday."

The image of Alberich pressed its hands to its head. "In name only! Everyone knows you're the real power behind the throne!"

Alberich turned pale. "That's me?"

Panopael patted him on the back. "Not lately."

The image behind Medelvae wavered, rippled, and stabilized again. This time, they could see an image of a water carriage streaking through the narrow streets of the Old City. As it sped through the Circle of the Well, a beggar – a girl younger than Panopael – rushed up to ask for alms.

Inside the carriage, a ghostly Filhardil jerked the controls, tilting the water carriage hard to the left. The sharp edge of the outer shell clipped the young girl across the chest, sending her sprawling onto the cobblestones.

The image of Filhardil chuckled. "Elves begging. It's disgusting."

The image of Panopael, snug in the backseat, shook her head. "Someone should do something."

Panopael recoiled from her own image, hiding her face.

The images faded, and Medelvae opened her eyes. "Days ago, deeds such as these would have determined your next destination. But by the time each of you made the Great Transition, you were choosing another path."

"That's true," Alberich said.

"In circumstances such as these, I am empowered to offer you a choice. You may stay here – between – or you may return to the Overworld for a time and allow your choices to tip the scales in one direction or the other."

"We can go back," Panopael said. "We can still stop Dokkalfar and Volundr!"

"Balance must be maintained, and values must be equalized," Medelvae said. "Reversing the Transition provides you with an invaluable opportunity to change the course of your existence. To pay for that opportunity, enormous sacrifice is required."

"Whatever it takes," Alberich said.

"We're ready," Panopael agreed.

"This is the payment: upon your return to the Overworld, each of you may lose the thing you value most."

Alberich frowned. "Can you be more specific?"

"Those are the terms," Medelvae said. "Choose."

Alberich stared at the ground for a moment; when he looked up, his eyes were sharp with certainty. "I'm going back."

Panopael nodded. "I'm going with him."

Medelvae walked to the edge of the crystal pool. " Walk into the water. Slip beneath the surface, and you'll be immersed once again in the dream of the world."

"It's that easy?" Panopael asked.

"The middle way is never easy," Medelvae said.

"Let's get on with it, then," Alberich said. He strode forward, took one step into the pool – and quickly withdrew, howling in pain.

"What?" Panopael asked. "What's wrong?"

Alberich gripped his calf. "It hurts! It's a trick!"

Medelvae was completely unfazed. "Pain is part of life. When you left the world, you were on the verge of great pain. When you return to the world, your pain will return."

"But I was fine before stepping into your poisonous pool!" Alberich insisted.

"There is no pain in the Underworld," Medelvae said calmly. "Only Sleep or Bliss."

"Let me get this straight," Panopael said. "When we go back to the world, we'll lose something valuable ... and we'll be in as much pain as we were when we left?"

"Of course."

Panopael walked to Alberich's side and held out her hand. "Come on. I'll go first."

Alberich, recovering slightly, shook his head. "No. We don't know what we'll face when we get back. I'll go first." He shrugged. "I'm king, after all."

Panopael started to protest, but Alberich would have none of it. He walked to the water's edge, crouched down, and turned to Medelvae. "Any way to make this easier?"

"When the time comes, I'll help you."

"Then I'll put my best foot forward," Alberich said, and, with that, he walked into the water. As it enclosed his ankles, he winced; as it rose to mid-thigh, he cried out. When the water encircled his waist, he collapsed from the pain, falling back on the shore, half-in and half-out of the water.

When he spoke, Panopael could barely hear his voice. "My legs ... they're broken. I can't ... they won't ..." He drew a sharp breath. "I could use that help, now."

While Panopael looked on, Medelvae put a cool hand on Alberich's forehead and, with a gentle push, sent him sliding under the surface. The instant the water closed over his head, he was gone.

Panopael took a deep breath. "My turn, I guess."

"So it is."

With only the slightest hesitation, Panopael dove into the pool and disappeared.

The Tarot of the Elves

Chapter Fifteen

> *Trump XV – The Devil.* "Volundr tempts Alberich with a false vision." *Shadow, falsehood, The Forbidden. Illusions and delusions. Emotional and spiritual blindness due to obsession with material pleasures. Indulgences and addictions.*

One moment, Panopael was suspended in crystal water; the next, she was once again tumbling through the air.

From out of nowhere, something tackled her. Sharp claws gouged through the fabric of her tunic and cloak, and the roar of the wind was replaced by the rhythmic beating of huge, leathery wings.

Panopael opened her eyes, and found herself locked in an airborne embrace with a dark-skinned Elsirin. At close range, the creature's stench was overwhelming; on the verge of vomiting, Panopael turned her head sharply to the side.

As she did, she saw a second Elsirin suspended in the air beside her. In its clutches, she saw Alberich, struggling and kicking. The beast tightened its grip, snapping the bones in one of Alberich's legs and prompting howls of agony.

As the creatures plummeted toward the ground, Panopael, too, decided to struggle. The Elsirin holding her responded with a swift kick, and its claw sliced cleanly through the fabric of Panopael's cloak, ripping the inner pocket apart and shattering the ornate box inside.

Panopael screamed.

Soon, she and the Elsirin were in the center of a cloud of fluttering Tarot cards, with the deck swirling around them like leaves in a summer storm. Panopael, heartbroken, clawed at the air, but in the end, every single card was caught up in the wind and carried away.

* * * * *

The Elsirin swooped through a window in the tower, tossed Panopael and Alberich onto an unforgiving stone floor, and flew back out into the night.

For several minutes, Panopael simply lay there, sobbing. The Tarot deck Taemerl had given her was gone; the Elsirin might as well have sliced out her heart and flicked it into the air. Medelvae had warned her: *You may lose the thing you value most.* But surely this price was too high. Without the cards, how could she go on?

With some effort, Panopael rose on one elbow and took in her surroundings. Overhead, an apparently endless spiral of beams and rafters twisted up as far as the eye could see. The surrounding walls, built of monstrous stones, were curved and featureless, giving Panopael the distinct impression she was at the bottom of a monstrous well. Beside her, face down on the floor, was Alberich.

The only light came from a few hissing, flickering torches pinned to the masonry. Their pitiful illumination revealed little: gray banners with red trim, a table laden with the Four Implements, and a massive throne carved from a single piece of slick, black stone.

Across the circular room, a door opened. Panopael hugged the floor and closed her eyes. She heard shuffling footsteps – a single person who moved to the far side of the room and began chanting in a language Panopael didn't understand.

Panopael risked a peek – and saw Dokkalfar. He stood with his back to her, facing the throne. Though she couldn't follow the words he spoke, his posture – head bowed, hands raised – told Panopael he was praying.

At that moment, Alberich began moaning very softly. His eyelids fluttered; an instant later, he was staring right at Panopael, his expression betraying a mixture of confusion and pain.

"Don't move," Panopael whispered. "Don't make a sound."

Alberich nodded, then closed his eyes.

When Panopael shifted her attention back to Dokkalfar, she noticed something new: the air around the throne was now suffused with what looked like boiling black steam. As she watched, the swirling wisps became thick tendrils of living smoke. Soon, she could see a dark silhouette near the center of the cloud – an indistinct man, sitting regally on the ebony throne.

As Dokkalfar's prayer grew louder, the figure on the throne became more and more solid. Suddenly, two bright red sparks appeared – the mysterious figure, opening its eyes.

As these flared to life, Panopael felt a sudden wave of nausea, and she forced herself to look away.

When the figure spoke, its voice was unimaginably deep. Its words rolled around the room, as though they seeped through the walls of the tower itself. "You no longer kneel when praying to me, Dokkalfar?"

Dokkalfar waved the comment away. "I've done everything you asked. You have the Four Implements. Keep your promise."

"I'm curious about this girl ... the one who almost defeated you."

"You said I would be king."

As their argument progressed, Panopael drew three deep, even breaths, calming her thoughts and centering herself. *I magicked myself from one place to the other once before,* she thought. *I wonder: can I do it again, and take Alberich with me?*

Without knowing quite what to do, she tried reaching out for Alberich – not with her hands, but with her feelings. At first, though she felt *something* happening, the results were indistinct and disappointing. Then, with an ease that surprised her, she was able to see Alberich with her inner eye: the red flare of pain along his legs and spine, the dark blue fog of fear that surrounded his head, and the dull, flickering embers of his life force.

Holding this image of him in her mind's eye as tightly as she could, she summoned all her remaining energy and channeled it into shifting the two of them from this place to anywhere else.

Suddenly, a familiar prickling spread from the crown of her head to the soles of her feet. *That's it!* she thought. *We're going!*

And then, just as abruptly, the envelope of energy shattered and fell away. A sudden loud hiss – like water thrown on hot iron – startled Panopael into opening her eyes.

The conversation between Dokkalfar and the dark figure had ground to a halt, and both of them were staring right at her. What stunned her even more than this was the floor of the chamber, where sizzling blue-white light now ran through a series of channels etched in the stone. From her position on the floor, Panopael couldn't see the entire design, but she could see enough to understand that she and Alberich had been placed in the center of a circle, and that the circle had somehow blunted her effort to escape.

"Even now, the girl you so quickly dismiss summons her powers ... and would have escaped, had it not been for me."

"You promised to make me king. You fulfill your promise, or I'll disperse you just as easily as I summoned you."

The dark figure laughed, exposing black, jagged stumps of teeth. "You might be surprised who summoned whom. I made you one promise, Dokkalfar: serve me, and you would unite the kingdom. But having failed to kill the current king, you are not a king ... and only the king may give me what I need." With that, he made a quick gesture, as though fanning away a fly, and Dokkalfar vanished.

The creature rose from his throne and came to stand at the edge of the charmed circle. "Panopael Mallir, your efforts honor me."

Panopael sighed and pulled herself into a sitting position. "Who are you?"

"Pick a name: Accuser, Slanderer, Rolinran, Lord of Illusions, Baal Davar. The Elves call me Volundr." He arranged his face into an expression of pity. "Your friend King Alberich is in great pain. Shall I heal him?"

"Why would you do that?"

"As a sign of my good intentions, of course. But I can take no action at all without your blessing, Panopael. Shall I heal him, or leave in him pain? The choice is yours."

Panopael considered this. "What's the price?"

"Did I mention a price?"

Panopael turned to Alberich. "I can see the pain in your legs and back. What do you want me to do?"

Alberich opened his eyes. He was pale and clearly suffering, but he managed a wry grin. "I always wanted to lie around doing nothing. Now I can, and no one can say anything about it."

Volundr sighed. "The pain is manageable now, but, in time, it will grow. It will prevent his sleep. It will consume his every waking moment. In time, every thought will blotted out by pain. All that will remain will be his memory of this moment – when you, Panopael, could have helped him, and chose not to take action on his behalf."

Panopael ran a hand through Alberich's hair. "If you can heal him, and you want to, then do; if you can't, or don't want to, then don't. But that choice is yours, not mine. He'll hate you; not me."

"I've got both the power and the desire," Volundr said. "But the Sleeping God has bound me. I can act, but only if you, Panopael, ask me to. In return, all I ask is that you convince your king to grant me free use of the Four Implements."

Panopael stood. "I'm sick of bargains and quests and gods and powers. I'll see Alberich home. I'll see Oberon and Alva restored. I'll get back home again to New Alfheimr. But I'll do all these things without your help."

"Perhaps I can change your mind."

Panopael whirled. "I said we're not interested in your –"

Words failed her. Volundr was gone. In his place stood Ellyll.

Chapter Sixteen

Ellyll, a vision in white, stood before them, her arms outstretched.

Panopael was instantly suspicious, but her heart gave a mighty leap, all the same. She squinted at the other woman, trying to spot the tell-tale aura that always accompanied illusory images. As far as Panopael could tell, this Ellyll was real. "Ellyll?"

Alberich, hearing his wife's name, struggled up on one elbow. In times past, he would have burst into tears; now, he clenched his jaw and held his head high. "Volundr, do you really think, after all we've been though, that an apparition of my wife can fool me?"

Ellyll put her hands to her face. "Alberich, I'm not sure how or why I'm here ... but please, listen to me. Dokkalfar and his treachery was just a diversion – an excuse to get you out of the city. The day you left, Dark Elves overran Alfheimr. The entire city has fallen. Taemerl and a few others are with me now, in the safe house, but its magic will not protect us much longer."

"That's not Ellyll," Alberich said. Even so, he continued to stare at her image, and Panopael could see the longing on the young man's face.

Ellyll held out her arms. "All our life together, you've depended on me. Now, I'm depending on you. I don't know what this Volundr creature is. I don't care. All I know is that Volundr says we can be all together, in a safe place, if you'll just give him what he wants."

"This won't work," Panopael said. "It's lame."

Ellyll wept. "We can sort this out later ... we can regroup and come up with a plan ... but we can't do that if we're not alive!" Suddenly, she pitched forward, falling to her knees and gripping her belly. A bright blossom of blood spread across the front of her white gown. "Alberich! The baby!"

The expression of disdain on Alberich's face faded, and he struggled to sit up. "Ellyll?"

Behind Ellyll, the air grew thick with dark swirls of smoke. They coalesced into the dark form of Volundr, who shook his head in pity. "Alberich, this is real."

Ellyll, now on her hands and knees, screamed her husband's name.

Tears streamed down Alberich's face. "What do I do?"

"Release the Implements," Volundr said. "You have no use for them. Give them to me, and I'll spare you and your family the horrors to come."

"Alberich," Panopael said, "Even if this is real, you just can't –"

Volundr merely flicked his fingers in Panopael's direction, but the force of his magic sent her sprawling. She rolled across the stone floor, landing in a miserable heap. As she scrambled to regain her feet, her right hand became tangled in the shreds of her ragged cloak. In the folds of torn fabric, she felt something familiar.

Panopael yanked her hand out of the ruined pocket, producing a single Tarot card: Trump XV: The Devil.

The card was crimped down the center, and one edge had been completely torn away. The illustration, though, was entirely intact: in the background, Volundr and Ellyll, and in the foreground, a hand holding Ellyll's amulet.

And there was something more – something Panopael had never noticed. Like the image of Erlkonig on the Death card, the entire illustration on the Devil card looked fake. The background was nothing more than a swirl of color; details were indistinct. In fact, the only aspect of the card that looked normal was the foreground: a hand holding Ellyll's glowing amulet.

Suddenly inspired, Panopael, suddenly inspired, burst into tears. "Alberich! What are you waiting for? Give Volundr the Implements and be done with it!"

Alberich, shocked, could barely speak. "What?"

"She's your wife, Alberich! Nothing else matters! Give him the implements and save her!"

Volundr raised an eyebrow, but looked pleased. "You should listen to your advisor."

Panopael ran across the room, took Alberich's face in her hands, and peered into his eyes. "Look at her!" Panopael screamed – and then, in a soft, low voice, added, "And then look at the amulet she gave you."

Alberich faltered. "Wha ... what?"

"The amulet," Panopael hissed.

"When the two of you are finally reunited ..."

"... it will gleam like the sun," Alberich said. He fished the amulet out of his collar. The untarnished pendant flickered, reflecting the torchlight ... but the sheen of the metal was entirely mundane.

Ellyll's eyes grew wide with terror. "Alberich! They're coming!" A gloved hand seized her hair and jerked her head upward. Another hand pressed a blade against the flesh of her neck. "I loved you!" Ellyll screamed. "Always remember it, Alberich! Even if you couldn't save us, I loved you so much!"

"It's not her," Alberich said.

"It's not her," Panopael repeated.

Ellyll vanished.

Volundr erupted into a rage, roaring and shrieking. "I'll keep you alive while I split open your hides! I'll dig tear your skinless bodies open and feast on your entrails! I'll rip your heads open and feed you fistfuls of each other's brains!"

Alberich made a face. "If he could really do all that, he would have done it by now."

"But he can't, so he wont." Panopael brushed a tear from Alberich's cheek. "Are you ready?"

He closed his eyes. "I'm ready."

Panopael stood, walked out of the charmed circle, and approach the table where the Four Implements lay.

Volundr froze. "The king must give the implements to me."

Panopael shook her head. "The Four Implements were given by the gods to the Elven people. They aren't yours. They're ours."

Volundr's voice was steady and even again – the very essence of reason. "Listen to me, Panopael. You've defeated me. You've exposed all my tricks. In the end, I have nothing left to tell you but the truth. Will you hear it?"

Panopael said nothing.

"Do you think I would just leave the Implements lying there, Panopael? Do you think I would fail to protect something so precious?"

Panopael, her hand over the Wand of Victory, hesitated.

"The Implements are enchanted, Panopael. If you touch them, you will die. But don't believe me; ask your intuition. Surely you can trust the voice within?"

Panopael's inner voice – never louder, never stronger – responded immediately. *Volundr speaks the truth.*

Volundr nodded. "You sense the truth in my words, don't you?"

Panopael frowned. There was something ... something on the edge of her awareness ... if she could just focus, just reason it out ...

And then, in the darkness behind Panopael's closed eyes, a vision appeared: a ring of twenty-two bright cards, spinning slowly in space.

Her inner voice explained: *You feared you had lost the Tarot forever; in fact, the cards are now a part of you.*

In the center of the ring, a single card appeared. Outlined in light, it drifted toward Panopael: the now familiar Devil trump.

At first, Panopael was perplexed. Her intuition told her Volundr was telling the truth, but the reading in her vision suggested deception. How could Volundr's statements be true and false ... at the same time?

Panopael raised her head, a ghost of a smile on her lips. "You're right. You are telling the truth."

Volundr smiled an eager smile. "I knew I could depend on your wisdom."

"The Implements *are* enchanted. But that's not something you've done. They've always have been enchanted; it's their nature. And if I touch them, I *will* die – but not *because* I've touched them. The fact is, we all die someday – or, at least, move on from this world to the next."

Volundr's smile faded.

"So, while your words are true ... your statement has only the illusion of truth. And I've had enough." Panopael lifted the Wand of Victory with both hands. "Goodbye, Volundr."

In Panopael's hands, the wand flared white-hot and began to hum. She lowered her voice, almost as if in prayer. "If it be the will of the gods, let me triumph over this enemy."

Panopael felt engulfed by rippling wave of heat; her hair stood on end, and the air around her crackled with energy. The gathering forced lifted her up off the floor, and then, finally, when she thought she could take it no more, a bolt of white-hot lightning flared upward from the tip of the wand. In the tower's uppermost recesses, thick beams and heavy stones splintered into millions of tiny shards.

The top of the tower blasted outward. Destructive energy cascaded down over the masonry walls, lapping at the stone like flame on kindling. The entire tower shuddered, knocking Panopael back into the charmed circle; the wand slipped from her hands and fell into a gaping crevice on the floor.

Volundr, eyes bulging, held his hands to his head, screaming.

Why doesn't he leave? Panopael wondered – and then, her intuition once again supplied the answer. *Bound in place by the Sleeping God.*

Debris rained down. A massive boulder tumbled down, striking the ebony throne and splitting it two. Volundr fell to his knees, clawing at his skull. Boils of searing light erupted on his smooth black skin. Finally, with every inch of his flesh ravaged by supernatural fire, Volundr exploded. Seconds later, there was nothing left of him but a rain of ash.

Panopael ran to Alberich, who opened his arms and shielded her as best he could. With sudden finality, the air overhead filled with a mighty roar. Blackness descended on them both, and in seconds, they were lost beneath a thundering downpour of wood and stone.

The Tarot of the Elves

Chapter Seventeen

Trump XVII – The Star. "With the implements in hand, Alberich finds the way home." *Hope, optimism, openness. Direction from above, guidance from divination. The light at the end of the tunnel. Resolution of worries and dissolution of fears.*

Panopael expected nothing but darkness – or, perhaps, her second glimpse of the Underworld in less than a day.

Impossibly, she and Alberich, still huddled together, were now outside in the open air. In the sky above, clouds were clearing and stars were peeking through. Around them lay a chaotic pile of rubble – the smoldering ruin of the tower.

Panopael blinked. "The tower fell *around* us?"

Alberich pointed at the ground beneath their feet. Surrounding them, shimmering with magical energy, was Volundr's circle of protection. "But what about the Implements?"

Panopael scanned the debris. "There." She picked her way over steaming ruins and collected them all: the wand, the cup, the sword, and the disc. The Wand of Victory, its energy spent for another thousand years, looked surprisingly mundane.

On the other hand, the cup, the sword, and the disc still gleamed.

Unscathed by the collapse, the three unused Implements looked as new as the day they the gods created them.

"It's over," Panopael said. "It's finally over."

"Not quite," Alberich said. "We've no idea where are, and no idea how to get back home."

Panopael considered this. "I could try to magic us home." She glanced around at the unfamiliar landscape. "Even back in the tower, I think I would have done better if I'd had some idea of where we were headed."

"I think that can be arranged," Alberich said, wincing as he sat upright. He nodded at the pile of implements at Panopael's feet. "Pass me the disc."

Panopael lifted it, a bit surprised at its weight. "You're going to use the disc to get directions home? Isn't that a little wasteful? I mean, you'll only be able to do this once every thousand years."

"I'm not just getting directions home. I'm getting the information I need to reunite the king and his seer with the people who need them most ... and getting the other two implements back to Alfheimr, where they can restore my parents to life." He took the disc from Panopael, gripped it tightly, and closed his eyes. "Show me what I most desire: the way home."

Immediately, the disc flared with an inner illumination. It seemed to spin in Alberich's hands, whirling and flashing, until finally, its center irised open. A shaft of silver light, as pure and clear as Panopael had ever seen, shot out of the heart of the disc and angled into the sky. Ultimately, it burst into a brilliant star: a single point of light. From this, a gentle radiance rained down, spotlighting a valley between two distant mountains.

Panopael memorized the location, aligning it with the stars overhead. In her memory, something clicked; they had seen those same mountains – The Ancestors – back when they had just entered the foothills of the Western Range.

With a mechanical click, the hole in the center of the disc snapped shut. Like the wand before it, the disc, its magical energy expended for another thousand years, looked almost mundane.

"Got what you needed?" Alberich asked.

"We're headed east, right through the Ancestors."

"Any reason to wait?"

Panopael shook her head. "It's past time."

They joined hands. Once again, Panopael prepared to draw on a rich and apparently inexhaustible reservoir of magic deep inside. She cleared her mind, focused her intention and –

"Stop!" Alberich shouted. "Do you hear that?"

Panopael, startled, took a moment to calm herself before cocking her head to one side to listen as carefully a possible. "I hear it, too," she said. "Someone moaning."

Alberich, unable to walk, pointed to a mound of rubble. "There."

Panopael dug through the debris with her bare hands. Finally, after using the Wand of Victory to pry a large stone away, she uncovered a pocket of open air. There, curled into a ragged ball, lay Dokkalfar. His face was smudged with soot, and his skin scratched and scraped; otherwise, he seemed unharmed.

He looked up at Panopael with pleading eyes. "Please – help me."

Panopael turned to Alberich. "Well?"

"I am Alberich, King of Alfheimr," Alberich said. "I do not leave men to die ... especially when I can bring them to justice."

When Panopael pulled Dokkalfar from the makeshift pit, he offered no resistance. Placing a hand on each of the men, Panopael pictured the safehouse in her mind.

In an instant, they were gone.

The Tarot of the Elves

Chapter Eighteen

> **Trump XVIII – The Moon.**
> "Ellyll stands at the city gates, longing for her husband."
> *Dreams, romance, the unconscious. Events that occur on a regular basis. Shorter cycles and phases. Intrigue and instincts. The allure of all things magical or fantastic. Welcome change.*

Ellyll lay in bed, unable to sleep.

The past few days had been as frantic as any she could recall. Work on the palace was progressing at a remarkable rate. The Elves of Alfheimr needed something to distract them from the terrible events of the past few days, and the goal of restoring the palace to its former glory inspired and occupied them all. Even with black mourning banners still flying, they had volunteered their physical labor and magical gifts, creating a unified workforce unlike any Ellyll had ever seen.

The real surprise, though, had come the day before, with the arrival of a contingent of Dark Elves from Fardaimr, far beyond the Western Range: five Elves, including the elderly King Restilaar.

* * * * *

In addition to dark news about the pitiful state of his own kingdom, Restilaar shared knowledge of a growing threat – a mysterious tower, a swirling magical barrier around it, and rumors of an ancient evil force struggling to free itself from exile. A number of Dark Elves had gone to investigate ... including Dokkalfar, the king's own son ... but had never returned.

"We are powerless, and our spirit has been broken," Restilaar had said. "Our resources are exhausted. Before this threat appeared, we were on the verge of opening our borders and begging for your aid and mercy. I propose we end the age-old divisions. If you will give our people access to food and healers, we will share our expertise in stone and metal work. Together, perhaps, we can push this thing back into the darkness from which it came."

"A truce?" Ellyll had asked.

At this, the old Elf had removed his crown and laid it on the table before her. "More than that. The children of the gods have been separated for too long. When we have conquered this threat, the people of both nations should be united under one rule: your husband's."

To Ellyll, the possibility of union had always seemed a dream. "Is such radical change possible?"

Restilaar laughed. "Ever look up at the Moon? That moon, with its waxing and waning, reminds us that change is the only constant. This change won't be easy ... but working together, I think we can achieve it."

They had been shaking hands when the first birth pangs came.

* * * * *

Ellyll slipped out of bed, crossed the room, and looked down into the ornate cradle where her new daughter lay. Her thin blonde hair gleamed in the moonlight. She had Ellyll's delicate features, but her ears, pointing in opposing directions – what King Oberon had always called "East-West Ears" – were definitely Alberich's.

Ellyll cleared her throat, rousing the Wolf that Velorl had insisted on assigning as her guardian. He snapped to attention immediately, padding over, his eyes and ears alert. Ellyll then lifted the baby, and, after ascending to the roof of the safehouse, floated gently upward.

The moon was fat and full. The Wolf flying alongside Ellyll eyed the bright sphere, and, after glancing up at his mistress for permission, saluted it with a long and hearty howl.

Finally, like feathers drifting to earth, Ellyll, her daughter, and the Wolf touched down just outside the city walls. There, as she had done every night since Alberich and Panopael's departure, Ellyll bowed her head and prayed to the gods for their safe return.

As she stood praying, a warm breeze grazed her cheek. Ellyll opened her eyes –and gasped.

For miles around, the landscape shimmered with unnatural light. Instead of the silvery, monochromatic tones of a moonlit world, Ellyll could see colors: the earthy stone of the city walls, pink buds on green trees, yellows and purples in the grassland flowers, and crystal blues in the nearby stream.

Ellyll glanced up. To the west, a shaft of blue-white light pierced the sky. At its tip was a single point of brilliant white light: a new star that burned brighter than any of the others, casting a celestial spotlight on the city of Alfheimr.

Ellyll broke out into a smile. Rocking from side to side, she looked down at her daughter. "Our prayers are answered, little one," she cooed. "Your father's coming home."

Chapter Nineteen

Trump XIX – The Sun. "The quest complete, Alberich and Ellyll are reunited." *Glory, energy, clarity. Dazzling success and overwhelming brilliance. Victory and delight. Openness and joy, warmth and expansiveness.*

Before the first light of dawn, the black and silver mourning banners disappeared from Alfheimr.

As the sun rose, its ruddy light revealed an entire kingdom swathed in the yellow and gold banners of royal celebration. Dazzling swags of brocatelle festooned the city walls. Flags fluttered from the tips of turrets, and the air was thick with the sound of trumpets and callahorns.

Elves from both Alfheimr and Fardaimr packed the streets, forming a noisy procession from the outermost reaches of the city to the Royal Ridge. Elves on horseback waved orange victory banners, and Elves on foot, holding sunflowers aloft, shouted and danced.

At the Royal Ridge, Elves crowded into the palace grounds. They climbed the trees and scrambled up the garden walls. They stood in he elaborate fountains, splashing each other.

When Velorl, the Priest, appeared on the steps of the palace, the crowd became suddenly solemn. The old Elf raised his hands in formal greeting, and, after donning a sayshell necklace, turned to address them.

"The dark times are past; disaster has been averted. As the nations are now united, so the royal couple is united once again!"

The crowd roared. The air reverberated with the force of their emotion, and their magical energy generated showers of spontaneous orange and purple sparks that burst in the sky like fireworks.

On cue, Alberich and Ellyll walked out of the towering palace doors. Alberich, his broken legs healed by Velorl just hours earlier, still walked with a faint limp, but his pride over the solar crown he wore was obvious in his step, and he greeted the celebrating Elves with a confident nod. Around his neck, he wore Ellyll's amulet; today, it gleamed like a second sun.

Beside him stood Ellyll, wearing the lunar crown of the High Priestess. She carried their daughter, who opened her eyes, surveyed the crowd, and responded with a long and satisfying yawn.

Velorl raised his hands again; the crowd again fell silent.

Alberich, his voice certain and steady, addressed the throng. "From the bottom of my heart, I thank you for the work you've done on behalf of the kingdom and my family. We returned in victory, but, by restoring the palace during my absence, you have made that victory complete. For this, I will be forever grateful.

"As you know, the Four Implements have been returned. Their great power is available to us only once every thousand years, and, in my quest, I drew upon one of them, the Disc of Desire, to find my way back here, to the family and kingdom I love with all my heart."

"A second Implement, the Wand of Victory, was used by a hero of the kingdom, who became my companion and advisor on this quest. I give you ... Panopael!"

The crowd picked up the name and chanted it: "Pan-o-pael! Pan-o-pael!" Wide-eyed and overwhelmed, Panopael peeked out from the palace doors. Led forward by Taemerl, she approached the king and queen and gave each a solemn bow.

"There is no gift that could possibly repay your bravery and service," Alberich said. "You have put aside your own needs; you have chosen to make our quest your own. To show our gratitude ... we could think of only one thing."

Ellyll stepped forward and, according to the ancient custom, raised her newborn child into the air with both hands. "People of Alfheimr ... I give you our daughter: the royal princess ... Panopael!"

The crowd's chant doubled in volume. Panopael bowed again; when she rose, her face was beaming with pride.

"Last night, after our return, the occasion came to use a third Implement," Alberich said. "As you know, my father, King Oberon the Wise, has long been the protector of the Implements, but has never used them on his own behalf. A terrorist act rendered my father into lifeless stone ... but now, the Sword of Consciousness has revived him."

Panopael didn't think the crowd noise could get louder – but it did, and this time, she could feel the noise of the celebration hammering at her like a physical force.

The palace doors opened, and King Oberon walked out to greet his subjects. As he approached, Alberich turned, removed the solar crown, and placed it on his father's head.

Oberon, his voice deep and rich enough to carry throughout the palace courtyard, stepped forward. "I am sorry I could not be with you during this dark time, but I am grateful that my son, Alberich, could take the reins and steer our country to victory. I am proud to have been chosen by the gods to serve you ... and I am proud that the gods have given me such a brave and faithful son."

As Oberon hugged Alberich close, the assembly raised their hands in silent salute.

"I am also grateful that, centuries ago, the gods entrusted the Four Implements to me. In all those years, I have never once used the Implements on my own behalf. But today, I confess to you that I have done so."

An excited murmur spread through the crowd.

"When Alberich told me that the Wand and Disc had been used in service to his quest ... and when I learned that he had wielded the Sword to restore me to consciousness ... I made a selfish decision. Using the Cup of Contentment, I took an action I felt was necessary to restore the soul of our kingdom."

When Oberon gestured to the palace doors, they opened to reveal Queen Priestess Alva.

Chapter Twenty

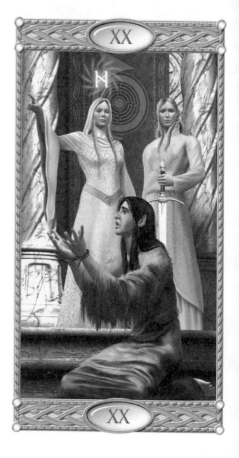

Trump XX – Judgement. "A resurrected Priestess Alva banishes Dokkalfar." *Revelation, analysis, examination. Waking up to the impact of past deeds, embracing the consequences of personal decisions. Being pronounced worthy or unworthy.*

As Alberich had crowned Oberon, Ellyll crowned Alva. The crowd's response – cheering, singing, dancing, and weeping – overwhelmed Panopael completely. For the first time she could remember, she wept tears of pure joy.

* * * * *

Back inside the palace, one last task awaited them. Oberon, Alva, Alberich, Ellyll, Panopael, and Taemerl took their places in the throne room. Moments later, Scarface entered the room; Dokkalfar, in chains, followed behind.

Panopael gasped. Dokkalfar's long hair was dull and matted. His face, at first, appeared unwashed, but Panopael realized with a shock that what looked like smudges were actually bruises. His robes, soiled with dirt and mud, hung in tatters.

Alva, standing in the Place of Judgment, didn't seem to find the prisoner's miserable condition surprising – a fact that shocked Panopael even more.

Panopael leaned closer to Taemerl. "What have they done to him?"

Taemerl gave the younger woman a grim smile. "He's a prisoner, Panopael. He's the murderer of the Queen Priestess. What did you expect?"

"Justice?" Panopael asked. "Mercy?" She looked at Dokkalfar and shuddered. "But I can't believe anyone deserves to be treated like this."

Taemerl nodded. "Look closer."

Panopael reluctantly looked back at Dokkalfar, who now kneeled before Alva. The fabric of the man's tunic had been split open several times by a vicious whipping; Panopael could see multiple wounds. Nauseated, she started to turn away; as she did, she noticed an odd detail: in the harsh sunshine pouring through the throne room's skylights, the edges of Dokkalfar's ragged robes were blurry and indistinct.

Without a word, Alva closed her eyes and summoned her powers. A whirling red glyph appeared in the air above her head, flooding the room with its baleful glare.

Panopael shielded her eyes with one hand. When the light faded, she spread her fingers and peeked between them.

Dokkalfar was still there. His hair, however, was sleek and clean. His face remained lean and angular, but the bruises were gone. His robes – no longer blurry around the edges – gleamed in the sunlight.

"As Priestess, I am One with the Truth," Alva said. "Your simple deceptions are a waste of our time and your energy, Dokkalfar."

As Panopael watched, the Magician looked down at himself, smirked, and stood. He straightened his shoulders, raised his chin, and clasped his hands behind his back. "So what will you do now, Priestess? Put on a show of tossing bones? Draw a circle and cast runes? Read the entrails of a dove?" He turned and looked directly at Panopael. "Draw a card or two, perhaps?"

Alva shook her head. "Do you deny that just days ago, you entered the Oraculum and murdered me?"

Dokkalfar laughed. "This is pure theater, and you know it. You also know the people of Alfheimr won't recover until they see a sacrifice ... so why not admit the truth, Truthseeker. I'm your scapegoat, aren't I?"

"Do you deny that you attempted to cast suspicion on Panopael Mallir, positioning her as my murderer?"

"And what will you do with me?" Dokkalfar asked. "Enchant me? Kill me? When did the gods give you power over life and death, Priestess?"

Alva, unfazed, continued. "Do you deny that you stole the Four Implements and sought to use them for selfish and evil ends?"

"Those same implements were used to free your husband and bring you back to life," Dokkalfar said. "When you're the beneficiary, extreme measures don't seem selfish, do they?" Dokkalfar folded his arms. "I am not a citizen of Alfheimr. I am not bound to your traditions. I do not recognize the authority of this court. Everything you're doing here today is done to soothe your own conscience, and I won't play along. Ban me. Enchant me. Kill me. But in the end, you'll know in your heart that instead of dispensing justice, you sought vengeance."

Panopael squirmed in her seat. "The nerve of this guy!"

Taemerl put a gentle hand on Panopael's arm. "Shhhh."

Alva smiled. "Dokkalfar of Fardaimr ... you speak the truth."

Dokkalfar's smirk faltered. "What?"

Panopael's jaw dropped. "What?"

"As your victim, and as someone who has suffered much grief due to your actions, I cannot trust my own judgment. Therefore, neither I nor any member of my family shall pass judgment on you."

Dokkalfar narrowed his eyes. "What's the trick?"

"There is no trick," Alva said. "Further, as you committed these deeds before the kingdom was united, your transgressions are not subject to the laws and customs of Alfheimr. Therefore, we cannot banish, enchant, or execute you."

"What, then? Let me rot in prison? Condemn me to forced labor?"

Alva gave Dokkalfar a look of honest pity. "Dokkalfar of Fardaimr ... I hereby set you free ... and hand you over to your father, the former King Restilaar."

A thunderclap shook the entire throne room; Panopael and others, startled, jumped despite themselves.

Restilaar – still in kingly robes, but no longer wearing a crown – appeared on the dais beside Alva and Alberich. The Dark Elf's eyes glowed red with anger, and the hand he extended to his son shook with barely contained rage. "Because of your actions, and for the betterment of our people, I forfeited dominion over Fardaimr. But I still hold authority over my own house, and I hold you, Dokkalfar, responsible for our current situation."

Dokkalfar looked like a trapped animal. "Father?"

It was the only word he managed before an invisible force swept him up and carried across the room.

The Tarot of the Elves

Chapter Twenty-One

> *Trump XXI – The World.*
> "Oberon, restored to life, accepts the four Implements from Alberich." *Completion, wholeness, fullness. The ending of a long cycle or phase of life. Having everything needed to thrive and be satisfied. Enlightenment.*

Dokkalfar, strangling, clawed at his throat and kicked his feet. When he landed in a heap at his father's feet, Restilaar lifted the younger Elf by the collar and shook him until he went limp.

"With your permission, Priestess ... my son and I will take our leave."

Alva bowed.

Black smoke, punctuated with red sparks, boiled up from Restilaar's feet. As the cloud closed over them, Dokkalfar managed to make a sound: a single, piercing wail that sounded more animal than Elf. An instant later, both Elves were gone.

* * * * *

The following day, along with hundreds of other Elves from the city, Panopael stood outside the Shrine of the Four Implements.

Alberich, looking handsome and royal, approached Oberon's throne;

after kneeling, passed the Implements one by one into his father's hands. Oberon gave Alberich a blessing, then summoned Velorl. The old priest approached, wrapped each Implement in an ornamental silk cloth, and, after placing all four in an elaborately carved case, retreated with them into the temple. The crowd cheered.

After all she'd been through, returning the Implements to their resting place struck her as slightly anti-climatic. Panopael, clapping with the rest, looked up at Taemerl. "That's it?"

Taemerl nodded. "Yes, I think that's –"

Oberon spoke, taking everyone, including Taemerl, by surprise. "Elves of Alfheimr! May I ask you to indulge me in one final thing?"

The crowd murmured, but came quickly to attention. Panopael glanced back at Taemerl and raised her eyebrows; the older woman shrugged and shook her head.

"As you know," Oberon said, "I have reigned over Alfheimr for more than a thousand years. When I took the post, I was a young Elf; today, though, I can feel the weight of the years on my bones."

No one stirred. Panopael could hear her own heartbeat in her ears.

"Long ago, I made a commitment to the gods and to you: to remain on the throne for as long I believed I was best equipped to rule the kingdom. But during these past few days of turmoil, I feel I've been given a sign. A new age has arrived ... and with it, there is a need for new leadership."

Oberon rose from his throne and stood beside his son. "Today, as we put the Implements to rest, it is time to put my reign to rest ... and to pass authority and power to someone who has proven himself worthy of our faith and confidence. The time has come to crown Prince Alberich King of the Reunited Lands."

All around Panopael, Elves – both light- and dark-skinned – jumped into the air, waved their hats overhead, and cheered. Panopael, though not entirely surprised, still found herself once again blinking back tears.

Alva summoned Ellyll, who rushed to her husband's side. As one, Oberon and Alva lifted off their crowns and placed them on the heads of their heirs.

Panopael joined the others, clapping and cheering. Overwhelmed with joy, she turned to embrace Taemerl ... but the older woman was gone. "Taemerl? Taemerl!"

Then, the now-familiar voice of her own intuition – which, she suddenly realized, sounded a great deal like Taemerl – resonated in her heart and head: *What was broken has been mended. What was missing has been found. What was needed has been given. The world is whole again.*

Panopael held her breath. Around her, the quality of the sunlight changed, becoming thinner and growing dim. The trees in the distance blurred and became indistinct, and the air around Panopael seemed to fold in upon itself.

Don't be afraid.

She turned and looked back at the royal family: Oberon, Alva, Alberich, Ellyll ... and now, in Ellyll's arms, the young princess Panopael.

Panopael tried to speak; no words came.

Alberich smiled at her and waved.

Panopael felt a burst of acceleration ... and then the entire world spun away into darkness.

The Tarot of the Elves

Epilogue

Panopael, her head still whirling, opened her eyes. At first, she saw only the exposed beams of the ceiling overhead.

She sat up and looked around. Cracked plaster over cold stone. Worn draperies. Splintery cabinets. Rickety shelves packed with dusty books. Creepy plants with leathery leaves and spiky vines. Tables covered with bottles and vials.

Grandmother Taemerl's house – *the safehouse.*

Panopael lay on a dusty couch in the corner of the great room, surrounded by furnishings that were familiar and strange all at once. Startled, she stood; immediately, she something tumbled out of her lap.

Looking down, she saw the ornate box of Tarot cards on the floor.

"Wake up from your nap?"

Panopael whirled. Taemerl – her gray hair twisted into long, old-style braids – stood just a few feet away, holding a candle. Her seamed face was twisted into a knowing smile.

"Taemerl!" Panopael snatched up the box, jumped off the couch, and ran to her grandmother, hugging the older woman as tightly as she could. "You made it back, too?"

"What are you going on about?"

"From Alfheimr! From the past! From the story in the cards!"

Taemerl laughed. "What a story!"

Panopael, suddenly serious, held her grandmother at arm's length.

"Don't do this to me, Taemerl. You tell me the truth. You got back years ago, didn't you?"

Taemerl stared into Panopael's eyes, as though looking for something. A few heartbeats later, she finally spoke. "Yes, Panopael. I got back home just minutes after I left. And I've been waiting for you ever since."

* * * * *

They spent the rest of the day pouring over the cards. Images that had been mute in previous days now spoke volumes, and Panopael went through the deck over and over again, asking questions and begging for stories.

Panopael picked up The Chariot. "Even though I was there, I'm not in any of the cards.

"Neither am I," Taemerl said. "But in a way, we're all in them, whether you can see us or not."

"Alberich looks like a hero all the way through – even when I was the one that saved him."

"Legends need heroes. Besides, in the end, the truth of a story isn't in the details, but in the truth it teaches."

Panopael gathered up the cards, squared them, and dealt a few onto the table. "You could have just told me all this."

Taemerl pointed a crooked finger at her granddaughter. "And would you have listened?"

Panopael laughed. "No."

Taemerl relaxed. "Some things can't be taught or told ... they have to be experienced."

Without warning, the front door burst open. Filhardil Mallir, his hat askew and his cloak billowing crazily around him, strode into the room, clapping his gloved hands together. "Gather your things. Time to go. Business calls." He stopped abruptly, staring down at the table. The tips of his ears turned red. "What's this?"

"Divination," Panopael said. "Tarot cards."

Filhardil pressed his lips together so hard they lost all color. "Mother, we discussed this."

Taemerl rolled her eyes. "Not often enough."

"Panopael, put those down. Wash your hands. Get in the carriage."

Panopael shook her head. "They're mine, and I'm taking them with me. And when my visit's over, I'll just magic myself home."

Filhardil's eyes bulged. "You'll do no such thing! Now get your books! Narnilor's called me! Work to do!"

"What work?" Taemerl said.

"Construction site," Filhardil said. "Found ruins. Shut down 'til I get there. Narnilor himself got involved, gods know why."

"Narnilor," Panopael murmured. "Why does that name –"

Taemerl cleared her throat. "In the old tongue, it means 'accuser.'"

Panopael shivered. She drew a card from the top of the deck: Trump XV, The Devil.

"I have many names," Panopael quoted. "Accuser ... Slanderer ... Rolinran." She gulped. "Rolinran ... Narnilor."

Filhardil all but yanked out his own hair. "Enough nonsense! I'll be late! Narnilor is not a patient Elf!"

"You said he was involved already," Panopael said. "Will he be at the construction site?"

"Narnilor? Leads by example. Always in the office. Never leaves the governmental tower."

Panopael said nothing. Instead, she gathered the cards, shuffled them again, and drew just one.

On it, Prince Alberich reclined against a sun-warmed rock, extending his hand to welcome a butterfly. His dog, a symbol of his instincts, dozed at his side.

At his feet, a black spider, hidden in plain view, crept ever closer.

The Tarot of the Elves

The Tarot of the Elves:

Structure and Story

The vast majority of Tarot decks published today contain a twenty-two card Major Arcana, plus a fifty-six Minor Arcana. The Minors are divided into four suits of fourteen cards each: ten numbered cards, plus four court (or "people") cards.

The Major Cards

In the *Tarot of the Elves*, the twenty-two Majors tell the story of young Prince Alberich. Sheltered and spoiled, he is completely unprepared for the chaos that arises when a Dark Elf murders the Queen Priestess Alva, enchants King Oberon, and steals the Four Implements – four sacred relics whose power can be summoned only once every thousand years.

His experience carries him along the "Hero's Journey" – a path that leads him from the innocence and inexperience associated with the Tarot's Fool card to the wholeness and enlightenment associated with The World. At each step along the way, he learns invaluable lessons about the nature, meaning, and purpose of life ... and, in the process, discovers the part he was always meant to play in the eternal struggle between darkness and light.

At the beginning of each chapter of Book II, the companion novel provides a brief entry from a "divinatory dictionary" – a reference work spelling out the keywords and meanings assigned to each of the Major cards. To learn more about a specific Major card, you can begin by reading this entry. Once you've done so, reading the corresponding chapter in the novel will help you see how the energies associated with the card are played out in Panopael's story.

The Minor Cards

In the *Tarot of the Elves*, as in most contemporary Tarot decks, the Minor Cards are divided into four suits: Wands, Cups, Swords, and Discs. These four suits correspond to the Four Implements: the Wand of Victory, the Cup of Contentment, the Sword of Consciousness, and the Disc of Desire. Specific themes or perspectives have been match to each of these suits:

Wands – intentions and ambitions
Cups – emotional and spiritual needs
Swords – intellect and analysis
Discs – physical needs and worldly desires.

Suit Card Symbolism

Within each suit there are ten numbered cards. The meanings assigned to each of these cards is not arbitrary; instead, it is determined by blending the theme of the suit with a very consistent system of numeric symbolism. Given the deck's heavy emphasis on myth and story, it's not surprising that the symbolic meanings assigned to the numbers 1-10 reflect ten "story points" found in most Western stories:

1 – The Inciting Incident
2 – Initial Resistance
3 – The Adventure Begins
4 – Early Success
5 – Unforeseen Complication
6 – Adjustment and Response
7 – Further Complication
8 – Decisive Action
9 – Climax and Closure
10 – Resolution and Outcome

For example: based on this system, on the Five of Swords, we would expect to see "an unforeseen complication" (Five) arise related to an intellectual or analytical process (Swords). In the illustration, we see what appears to be a demented young Elf wreaking havoc and committing murder. In the Swords story, these events are, in fact, unforeseen complications of a father's decision to bring the boy back from the dead.

In addition, each suit also contains four court (or "people") cards: a Page, a Knight, a Queen, and a King. Each office of the "royal court" is associated with specific actions and attitudes:

Page – Learning or Discovering
Knights – Acting or Doing
Queens – Feeling or Encouraging
Kings – Controlling or Directing

The meaning assigned to a court card is determined by blending the theme of the suit with the actions and attitudes of a court office. For example: on the King of Cups, we see Masrael, a young Elf who must control (King) his emotions (Cups) and wait patiently for his fiancée to discover the error of her ways.

The Legends behind the Minors

Some prefer to "decode" card meanings using a combination of suit and number symbolism; others prefer to depend entirely on intuition. Either of these methods may be used with the *Tarot of the Elves*.

However, it's also true that each suit recounts one of four legends revealing how wise King Oberon came to possess the Four Implements. If you know these stories, you can apply their wisdom to you life ... and enhance the depth and clarity of your reading by using story moments as fuel for your intuitive process.

To further enhance your work with the deck, this section also provides keywords and insightful notes on every Minor card.

The Suit of Wands
Selomir and the Wand of Victory

The Dark Elf Selomir spent his days following his passion: collecting rare and unusual crystals from the volcanic regions along the Western Range. One day, while scouting for crystals, he was shocked to see a spectral hand offering him the mysterious and powerful artifact all Elves recognized as the Wand of Victory (1).

Even as Selomir took hold of the Wand, Volundr, an ancient and powerful spirit, tried to claim the Wand for himself (2). Selomir won the confrontation, then took possession of the Wand and used its power to advance his selfish desires. Against the will of the Elves of Alfheimr, he stole the throne from young King Oberon (3) and forced an Alfheimran girl, Uulanel, to marry him

(4). The Elves of Alfheimr, led by a passionate young Elf named Fallodar, rebelled against Selomir, and a bloody civil war ensued (5).

Supported by the power of the Wand of Victory, Selomir quelled the uprising and claimed the entire world as his own (6). With time, though, because none of his victories had been won through his own skill or effort, his achievements rang hollow (7).

Selomir rid himself of the wand (8), returning the kingdom to Oberon and releasing Uulanel from forced marriage (9). Eager to return to work that fulfilled him, Selomir went back to what had always made him happy: gathering crystals to fashion into jewelry of his own design (10).

Ace of Wands

New Direction

The appearance of the Ace suggests that an opportunity to change direction is coming your way. Are you willing to make a change and accept the responsibility that comes with it? If not, perhaps you should stick with the tried and true.

Selomir already has a wand in hand, indicating that he already has a direction and purpose in mind; when you are confronted by new options, you must decide whether to embrace change or continue along your current path. Selomir's backpack is full of harvested crystals; if you decide you need a change of pace, what will you do about your existing obligations?

A spectral hand – a symbol for the forces of fate or the will of the gods – offers Selomir the Wand of Victory. Be mindful that this moment in your life is part of a larger plan; the decisions you make have ramifications beyond the immediate future.

Questions to Consider: If you could have whatever you wanted now, what would it be? What small step can you take today toward realizing your larger goal?

Two of Wands

Difference

Here, Selomir wrestles with an ancient evil spirit, Volundr – the Elven counterpart to the Western concept of the Devil or the Shadow. Volundr embodies the internal doubts and external critics we encounter whenever we pursue positive change in our lives.

In situations like these, we tend to think in terms of extremes: pros and cons, A or B, one option or the other. Comparing and contrasting your options emphasizes the differences among them ... but don't forget that this decision may not require an "all or nothing approach."

You can minimize conflict and maximize success by thinking in terms of balance. Where's the middle ground? Single-minded pursuits usually result in loss (Selomir's overturned bag of crystals) and stress (Selomir's attitude). That said, if you're absolutely certain you're right, stick to your guns – even if the Devil himself opposes you.

Questions to Consider: What objective evidence could support my beliefs or decisions? What does the opposition have to say ... and how might an opposing viewpoint expand my perspective?

The Tarot of the Elves: Structure and Story

Three of Wands

Implementation

The triangular motif on the wall reinforces this card's association with the number three, which is symbolic of the movement from deliberation to action. Here, Selomir has used the Wand of Victory to ascend to the throne – not by virtue of his own merit, but through the employment of supernatural force.

For you, the time has come to act ... but with action comes responsibility. Are your actions right? Are they called for? Are they being taken with everyone's best interests at heart? Implementing a selfish plan may advance you quickly ... but even the Elves believe in karma, and, eventually, a self-centered approach may backfire severely.

Note Selomir's pose, which suggests aggression. As you move forward, be careful to do so in ways that encourage cooperation instead of opposition. Note, too, young King Oberon's submissive posture. Sometimes, moving ahead requires us to step back or step down. Leading and doing are two different things; don't confuse them.

Questions to Consider: How can you go from thinking to doing? How certain are you that your actions are best for everyone involved?

Four of Wands

Achievement

Don't you love it when a plan comes together? Selomir certainly does – but look at the impact his achievements have had on those closest to him. What should be a celebration has the emotional tone of a funeral ... all because Selomir has achieved his victory at the expense of others.

If you've recently achieved something, this card can be a reminder to celebrate that achievement in an appropriate way. Such celebrations don't have to be elaborate, but they are important; if you don't mark milestones as you pass them, how will you measure your progress along life's path?

Keep your eye on the goal; at the same time, be aware of how your progress is impacting others. If you win – and this card suggests you may well do so – how can you make this victory into a "shared victory?" What benefits will your success offer others who might be inclined to celebrate with you?

Questions to Consider: How aware are you of the emotions and responses of the people around you? To what extent might you be too self-absorbed to notice their needs?

Five of Wands

Conflict

Don't let the violence depicted in this card's illustration cause you to turn away from an important lesson: when we become angry, when we force our way forward without regard for the feelings of others, and when selfishness and ambition blind us to the consequences of our actions ... people around us get hurt.

Selomir's stolen crown is askew; the kingdom and the good of its people is literally no longer "on his mind." His self-centered focus has launched a terrible conflict, and a battle rages all around him. His only response? To fuel the fire of chaos by applying even more force.

Conflict is coming – but you don't have to be a passive victim, waiting to be swept away by a shockwave of crisis. First, evaluate your own actions. How have you contributed to the fray? Then, remember your goal. How can you keep yourself (and others) focused on what you really need to achieve?

Questions to Consider: What's the difference between desire and greed? What can you do to temper your emotions and actions ... and make the way smoother for everyone involved?

Six of Wands

Victory

Selomir stands at the summit of the highest point in the Western Range, master of all. He's won the battle. He's won the war. He's won the world. This card, then, can herald great victory and advancement for you ... but it should also serve as a sobering reminder that, especially for those who act irresponsibly, it's lonely at the top!

In the valley below, the survivors of the great battle bow down to Selomir. He's captured the flag ... but has he captured their hearts? Are the people around him obeying because they want to ... or because they have no other choice? There's a difference in a Lord and a Leader. Which do you aspire to be?

If your victory has already arrived, celebrate it ... but remember, too, that the pendulum is already swinging. Having ascended to such great heights, there's only one direction left to go. If you've treated others with respect and kindness, then your descent back to earth can be almost as pleasant as your rise to greatness.

Questions to Consider: How can you make the most of your current success? How can you use the power you have in responsible ways?

Seven of Wands

Restlessness

Selomir, having conquered the world, sits on Oberon's throne. His crown is missing; having realized his goal, being king is literally no longer "on his mind." The wand in his hand is not as radiant as before. The offerings at his side – a fortune in jewels, plundered from the livelihood of others – mean nothing.

Sometimes, attaining a goal is simply not as exciting as working toward it. In your case, it's likely that you've finally achieved a goal ... but now, having achieved it, you don't feel as satisfied or happy about it as you thought you would. You're restless. Instead of being satisfied, you're asking, "What's next?"

This, then, is a dangerous time for you – because, in your boredom, it's all too tempting to stir the pot, just to keep yourself occupied. If you can come up with good reasons to change things, do so ... just be sure you're acting out of a genuine desire to move forward. Take care not to let "itchy feet" lead you down a disastrous path.

Questions to Consider: What's the next logical step? How can you make the most productive use of this time? When's the last time you examined your long-term goals?

Eight of Wands
Change

Attaching a letter of confession and regret, Selomir rids himself of the Wand of Victory. In the distance, the sun sets, reflecting the fact that Selomir's desire to rule has left him. Meanwhile, the wand he once fought for is sent sailing through the air, representing a decision to release all assumptions and intentions.

When this card appears in a reading, it's often a harbinger of news and minor upheaval. Change is constant; rather than fight it, you'd do well to embrace it. Without change, we stagnate and die. And while it's true that change and loss often go hand in hand, there are often things in our lives that need to be swept away.

By releasing our death-grip on an outdated plan, we free ourselves to be brought back to the path the gods intended for us. When we toss aside the wand of our own intentions, we make room for grace to lead us to a new and unexpected state of being.

Questions to Consider: How can I peacefully embrace "letting go?" What can I do to tell the Universe I'm ready for change? To what extent is there something I need to confess or apologize for in order to move on?

The Tarot of the Elves: Structure and Story

Nine of Wands

Attainment

From out of the blue, the Wand of Victory – long the implement of their oppression – falls from the sky. Its release frees Uulanel from a sham marriage and returns King Oberon to his rightful place as the ruler of Alfheimr. This is a time of attainment: being given what you've been working for.

As you work toward a goal, you may suffer resistance and setbacks. At some point, though, if you persevere, you'll begin to see real progress. If you've worked to put yourself in the right place at the right time, the goal you seek may well fall right into your lap.

Note that Uulanel and Oberon, having read Selomir's note of apology and confession, are more focused on progress than punishment. As good fortune shines down on you, remember the role mercy should play in your life; one way to thank the Universe for its gift is to extend charity and credit to others.

Questions to Consider: What will I do when I finally get what I want? How can I, even in success, remain humble and attuned to the needs of others?

Ten of Wands

Labor

In traditional decks, the Ten of Wands often depicts a bent figure stumbling forward under an unbearable load of bundled sticks. Readers often associate it with depression and despair, and warn those they read for that the future holds terrible burdens and unpleasant consequences.

Here, then, we might be surprised to see Selomir smiling and happy, making his way through the Western Range, gathering crystals once again. His wand – not the one taken from the gods, but the one he carved for himself in childhood – is budding with new growth. His expression is a happy one.

Hard work toward a goal we care about need not be backbreaking labor. When our work is informed by a love for ourselves, a love for others, and a love for what we do, then even very difficult, unattractive, or too-familiar tasks can be taken on with a spirit of joy. Today, simply by doing what you're asked to do, you may experience remarkable new growth.

Questions to Consider: Am I prepared to work for what I want? How do I feel about hard work and practice? How often do I allow myself to experience the joy of focused work?

Page of Wands
Challenge

Upon first discovering the Wand, Selomir had to learn how to wield its power to make his desires into realities. That process required time, patience, a willingness to experiment, and an ability to remain enthusiastic, even in the face of repeated failures.

As seen on the Page, Selomir has a confident stance, but lacks the true confidence that arises when we successfully overcome the obstacles fate puts in our path. And don't forget: while Selomir eventually learned enough about the Wand to rule the world, his victories ultimately felt hollow because he, himself, had not ascended to power by meeting challenges of his own.

This card points to a person who tends to be more enthusiastic than talented, or more confident than experience will warrant. If the card applies to you, it may be a warning that challenges are coming. Will you have the stamina to pass the test?

Questions to Consider: If my situation is a test, what skills can I deploy to beat this challenge? How can I act more confident in the face of challenges?

Knight of Wands

Excitement

Here, Fallodar, the zealous young Elf who suffers a terrible defeat on the Five of Wands, charges into battle. He is caught up in the passion of the moment; the excitement of leading a battle has unbalanced him. He rushes forward, helter-skelter, propelled more by a zeal for glory than a head for strategy.

We crave excitement, and some measure of it can engage or relax us. But an addiction to excitement works against us. In this image, Fallodar's excitement – symbolized by the swirling fall leaves – leaves him dizzy and distracted. That's not a good frame of mind for a soldier!

This card points to a person who tends to be more reactionary than reflective, or more excited than the situation warrants. If the cards applies to you, you'd do well to calm down, take a few deep breaths, and see how the situation looks when your mind is fresh and your thoughts are focused.

Questions to Consider: What gets me excited? How do I act when I'm excited? How does excitement impact my decision-making? When is excitement appropriate?

Queen of Wands

Submission

Rather than resist the edicts of King Selomir, faithful Uulanel bowed to his commands and entered a loveless marriage. In doing so, she shows her respect for the laws that govern Elven civilization and culture – respecting the office, even if she could not respect the man occupying it.

Some will see submission as a sign of weakness, but true submission – setting one's own desires aside for the good of others – requires enormous restraint and discipline. In this image, Uulanel grasps a glowing wand – a reminder that, even in submission, she remains true to the values that motivate and define her.

If you've drawn this card, it's time for you to consider the value of submission in your own circumstance. Is there a way to embrace what you're resisting? You might also consider how submission to a discipline – a diet, a practice schedule, an exercise program – might actually become the key to meeting your long-term goals.

Questions to Consider: How do I feel about submission? To what or to whom do I currently submit? How might submission be the key to victory?

King of Wands

Responsibility

In this image, young King Oberon grasps the Wand of Victory. Selomir has exhausted its power, destroying the world in the process. Even so, in Oberon's hands, the Wand will now become a symbol capable of uniting the Elves of Alfheimr and inspiring them to rebuild.

In taking hold of the Wand, Oberon reassumes responsibility for the fate of his people and the state of his nation. As King, he does not have the luxury of blaming others for his success or failure; instead, he accepts the mantle of authority and all the personal responsibility that comes with it. While willing to hear the counsel of good advisors, Oberon also knows that important decisions are strictly his to make.

This card often points to a person who needs to take responsibility for his or her own actions, or may stand for someone who tends to respond to a crisis by stepping into a leadership role.

Questions to Consider: Who's responsible? How can you be more responsible? In your situation, what would it mean to take responsibility?

The Suit of Cups
Hallavae and the Cup of Contentment

Hallavae, an Elven maiden, was bathing with her friend and suitor, Masrael, when a spectral hand offered her the Cup of Contentment (1). Thinking the Cup would show her an image of Masrael, Hallavae asked it to reveal her perfect mate. At that moment, Hal'lael, a perfect masculine reflection of Hallavae, appeared. Hal'lael loved everything Hallavae loved, dreamed everything Hallavae dreamed, and was exactly like Hallavae in every way (2). Much to Masrael's disappointment, Hallavae and Hal'lael were soon wed (3).

Because both Hallavae and Hal'lael were exactly alike, each could perfectly anticipate the actions and reactions of the other; soon, their relationship grew predictable and dull (4). But because Hal'lael also shared Hallavae's tendency to blame others for personal misery, soon, the two were constantly fighting (5). Ultimately, this led them to the realization that the most satisfying relationships are based more on an appreciation for differences than an obsession with similarities (6).

With help from the Priestess Pretsea, their enchanted relationship was dissolved (7). Hallavae, having learned her lesson, left the Cup behind with Pretsea (8), who passed it on to King Oberon (9). Hallavae returned to Masrael and, appreciating him all the more, went on to establish a happy family with him (10).

Ace of Cups

Attraction

Aces connect with opportunity, and, in this case, you are likely already feeling the emotional attraction of an open door that you consider new and appealing. The Ace invites you to consider the extent to which this opportunity might be to your benefit and advantage ... and also to ask yourself, "Why is this thing so appealing?"

In the picture, Hallavae is just reaching for the Cup of Contentment; as yet, she hasn't activated its power. Along these same lines, you aren't yet obligated to accept the cup that life is now offering you. At this point, you're still free to embrace or reject this opportunity. You'd do well to consider the pros and cons of all possible courses of action.

Note, too, the fear and caution on poor Masrael's face! Be aware that the things that attract you may repel others ... sometimes with good cause. Before pursuing what you believe would make you content, why not consult with those who will be most impacted by your choice?

Questions to Consider: What do you really want? What are the pros and cons of the choices available to you? What qualities must something have to attract you?

Two of Cups

Empathy

Hallavae expected her question ("Who would be my perfect mate?") to summon an image of Masrael, her fiancé. Instead, the Cup's enchantment generated Hal'lael, a perfect masculine reflection of Hallavae.

In some ways, then, the Cup understood Hallavae better than she understood herself, empathizing with her deep-seated need for affirmation and companionship. And certainly Hal'lael, as masculine mirror of Hallavae, would feel a deep and abiding connection with her.

The appearance of the Two of Cups, then, is an invitation to feel something as others must feel it ... to see your situation from the perspective of another. How closely can you empathize with a radically different viewpoint? How easily can you set subjectivity aside ... and seek out common ground?

Questions to Consider: What do the people involved in my situation have in common? With whom do I easily empathize? How important is empathy?

Three of Cups

Dedication

Beneath an arch of celebration, Hallavae and Hal'lael declare their undying affection for each other. In Elven culture, this act is not taken lightly, for Elves tend to stay with one mate for the entirety of their sojourn in the world. This sort of commitment requires great dedication – a sincere desire to place the needs of another over the needs of the Self.

When we dedicate ourselves to one person, organization, idea, faith, or course of action, we must often neglect another. Masrael, standing alone in the background of this card, serves as a reminder that dedication to one often calls for the abandonment of another.

Finally, as those who know the story already know, Hallavae's dedication of herself to Hal'lael was sincere, but misguided. Over time, experience may prompt us to revisit the people and causes we've aligned ourselves with; doing so is both natural and healthy.

Questions to Consider: What are you personally dedicated to? What are the consequences of your choices? How certain are you that the person or idea you are aligned with is worthy of your dedication?

Four of Cups

Listlessness

Because Hallavae and Hal'lael were perfect reflections of each other, each could perfectly anticipate the other's thoughts, words, and deeds. While this seemed delightful at first, with time it leeched the element of surprise from their relationship, leaving them bored and listless.

In the image for the Four of Cups, clouds loom overhead, indicating that a storm is gathering, but has not yet broken. Meantime, an eerie stillness descends. There is no freshness in this moment; the energy of this scene – and this card – is stagnant and stale.

When you draw this card, you may find that what once delighted you no longer does, or you may be realizing that something you valued in times past no longer appeals to you. In your soul, you know it: instead of moving forward, you're just carrying on ... and your craving for something new is growing.

Questions to Consider: How can you move from boredom to action? At what point did you make the transition from delighted to dulled? Can your feelings be reversed ... or is it time to move on?

Five of Cups

Discord

With no differences to spice their interaction, both Hallavae and Hal'lael went on to experience the natural product of unmitigated boredom: discord. Each is still a mirror of the other ... but now each is also a mirror of the other's contempt, and the potential for spiteful action is doubled.

The bolt of lightning emphases how suddenly discord can arise. The altar in the background features an inverted star, suggesting that rational thought has been abandoned. At the heart of Hal'lael and Hallavae's struggle is the Cup of Contentment – the very thing that, just days ago, prompted their union.

In your own situation, you may face any of a number of manifestations of discord, from petty arguments to barely concealed contempt. This is a volatile time, and you'd be wise to monitor your own words and actions closely. If others lose control of their emotions, do your best to keep a cool head.

Questions to Consider: What's the basis for the disagreement? How can you create a win-win outcome? What feelings need to be expressed?

Six of Cups
Mutuality

Their issues resolved, Hallavae and Hal'lael finally reach an unexpected agreement: they decide to part company. While this may strike us as a sad outcome, we must remember that their decision is a mutual one. At this point, each is once again focused on meeting the needs of the other, and the two share a single goal.

The presence of the Priestess Pretsea reminds us that sometimes, in order to see past our own biases and achieve mutuality with another, we need the assistance of a third (and more objective party). In order to see eye to eye, we may also have to set our strongest emotional reactions aside – a fact illustrated here by the placement of the Cup on the sacrificial altar.

In your situation, there is a real need to emphasize what you and others have in common. If there is a need, meet it. If there is a request, grant it. If there is a question, answer it. To achieve mutuality – a true union of spirit – set aside your differences and take others' needs as seriously as you take your own.

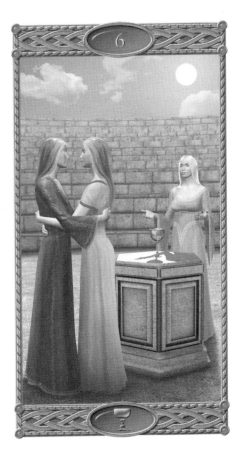

Questions to Consider: How can I cultivate a better understanding of others? How can I encourage others to show me respect and empathy?

Seven of Cups

Illusion

Here, Priestess Pretsea draws upon her own powers of Truth to dispel the illusory character of Hal'lael. Before Hallavae's eyes, the "mirror image" is reduced to watery residue, dissolving their relationship. This is a painful thing for Hallavae – but it is also a good thing, and she leaves the situation sadder but wiser.

We all tend to cling to our illusions; sometimes, we feel as though we have nothing else to keep us going. We tell ourselves that our illusions are vital to our happiness and well-being. We sometimes prefer the soft focus of the dream world to the harsh lines of reality.

Today, though, you would do well to distinguish between what is real and what is not. Ask yourself: is what I believe objectively true? Can it be proven? As you strip illusion away, you will come face to face with your own reality ... and this is an important step on the road to growth and wholeness.

Questions to Consider: What illusions do I cling to? What is the truth of my situation? How can I be more realistic and objective?

Eight of Cups

Loss

With Hal'lael now nothing but a memory, Hallavae turns her back on the Cup of Contentment and walks away into a spectacular sunset. In moving from empathy to detachment, she has come full cycle, and now she can return to her world with greater objectivity and full involvement.

The sunset on this card reinforces the fact that all things end ... but it also reminds us that all endings are part of a larger cycle of loss and renewal. In the foreground, we see the watery remains of Hal'lael; in times of change, we would do well to embrace the idea that some things, having slipped through our fingers, cannot be restored.

When your heart is aching, it can be difficult to focus on the future. Still, you must find a way. The past is lost forever, and the present moment is the only reality. Rather than dwell on what has been lost, why not focus on what can be?

Questions to Consider: What have I lost? To what extent is that loss reversible? How can free myself from regret and move on?

Nine of Cups
Morality

When Hallavae departs, the Priestess Pretsea finds herself in possession of the Cup of Contentment. Rather than keep this otherworldly talisman for herself, she does what is best for the Elven people ... and presents it to King Oberon for safekeeping.

As we gain increased access to great amounts of trust, wealth, or power, doing the right thing becomes more and more important. But what dictates morality? In order to bring ourselves into alignment with the will of the gods, we must do some soul-searching. We have to discover what our values are, and, once we discover them, we must choose to live by them, even when doing so is inconvenient.

Pretsea could have kept the chalice; she was under no obligation to give it to the king. In your situation, you are free to take any action you choose. In the end, though, you are going to have to live with your choices. Is any profit worth losing your respect for yourself?

Questions to Consider: Who am I when no one is looking? What values guide my actions? How moral am I?

Ten of Cups
Fulfillment

Beneath a rainbow (the symbol of promise), Hallavae and Masrael are depicted as the couple they were always meant to be. Hallavae, having learned to value reality over fantasy, is now free to be truly fulfilled by her imperfect – but much loved – family. In embracing what truly is, she finds she has everything she needs.

A good relationship is hard work. A vibrant faith requires daily nurturing. A bright spirit must be supported with the disciplines of meditation and right action. This kind of maintenance is hard work, but necessary work. Unless your affection motivates action, it is unlikely that any relationship (with people, Elves, or gods) will ever be fulfilling.

Let this image of happiness inspire you. Through prayer, meditation, and action, allow yourself to be led to what truly fulfills you. Once you taste true fulfillment, no pale, watered-down illusion will ever distract you again.

Questions to Consider: What actions leave me feeling completely happy and content? What people help me be my very best self? What truly fulfills me?

Page of Cups
Curiosity

Here, Hallavae admires the Cup of Contentment. Her mind whirls with possibilities; her heart pounds with anticipation. She's heard stories about the Cup all her life; now, she holds it in her hands. In her situation, how would you feel?

In this illustration, Hallavae is surrounded by lush greenery – a symbol of growth and potential. At her feet, we see a rushing stream – a symbol of the noise and constant change associated with life. Channeled properly, our curiosity leads to growth, prompting investigations into things we don't fully understand. If we ignore our curiosity, we remain sealed in an unchanging world, but if we give in to it, our world becomes a more complex place.

This card suggests someone is curious; given the theme of this suit, that curiosity is often associated with love, sex, new feelings, or spiritual matters. It may also recommend a strategy: try to see your situation with fresh, new eyes.

Questions to Consider: What do I need to know more about? What would a beginner do in my situation?

Knight of Cups
Enticement

In the Tarot of the Elves, the Knight of Cups is Hal'lael, the enchanted, masculine mirror-image Hallavae summons with her wish for a perfect mate. He is an ideal figure, composed of pure emotion. Here, he entices us to step into the turbulent water and embrace his perfection.

He looks good – from a distance. As we drawn nearer, though, we begin to see his imperfections – and our own. Fantasy is one thing; reality is another. At some point, the former gives way to the latter, and we discover that having something is not quite as pleasurable as simply being enticed by it.

The Knight of Cups often represents someone who is being enticed – a person who feels a strong emotional urge to take action *now!* It may also suggest a strategy: analyze carefully what entices you ... and remember to see that person, situation, or event as realistically as possible.

Questions to Consider: What about this person or situation is attractive? To what extent are emotions dictating my actions?

Queen of Cups
Enlightenment

The Priestess Pretsea is an Elven wise woman, empowered to see and hear The Truth in any words or situations. Her clarity comes from within. Having dedicated herself to the pursuit of What Really Is, she knows that her emotions are little more than turbulence on the surface of the water. Given time and patience, these ripples will fade, and her depth will remain.

This unusual degree of self-knowledge gives the Priestess a level of insight that can, in the eyes of the unenlightened, seem almost supernatural. Enlightenment, however, is available to all of us, if we will dedicate ourselves to the practice of focus and restraint.

The Queen of Cups usually connects with someone who possesses great spiritual and emotional insight. As a strategy, it may recommend that you seek out the counsel of someone with more spiritual or emotional maturity than you. If you are not yet as evolved as a Priestess ... the next best thing is to know where to find one.

Questions to Consider: What can I do to calm and center myself? Who is the most emotionally stable and spiritually evolved person I know? What would this person do in my situation?

The Tarot of the Elves: Structure and Story

King of Cups

Restraint

When Elven children fidget and grow impatient, mothers are likely to say, "Remember Masrael." When his own true love sought solace in the arms of an enchanted being, Masrael could have become angry or violent; instead, he restrained himself ... and waited patiently for the situation to resolve itself.

Here, Masrael sits and waits for Hallavae to return. Behind him, a flaming wand reminds us that he has his own agenda; he does not, however, allow that agenda to prompt rash action. At his feet is the Cup of Contentment – but rather than use that cup to achieve his goals, he prefers to see what he can achieve with faith and patience.

The King of Cups points to a person who is capable of controlling his or her emotional responses ... or, alternatively, to someone who needs to learn to do so. As a strategy, the card recommends reeling in your feelings, sucking up your fears, and waiting patiently to see how the situation will evolve.

Questions to Consider: How can I achieve better control of my feelings? What will happen if I am patient and wait?

The Suit of Swords
Calivan and the Sword of Consciousness

One dark night, a proud and powerful Elven priest named Calivan was researching forbidden knowledge in hopes of finding the key to bringing his departed wife, Isovel, to life (1). During these secret studies, a spectral hand appeared and offered Calivan the Sword of Consciousness. Calivan, proud to be chosen, agreed to guard the Sword with his life.

That night, a vicious Dark Elf burst into Calivan's home. He held Calivan's son, Galibrech, hostage, promising to spare the boy's life if Calivan would turn over the Sword (2). Calivan refused, protecting the Sword ... but losing his son in the process (3).

Using the forbidden knowledge he had gained, Calivan used the Sword to reanimate his son (4). Galibrech, though, was tainted by the touch of death and could not be controlled (5). His misdeeds soon forced the city elders to banish both Calivan and Galibrech (6).

One morning, while Calivan meditated, Galibrech stole away with the Sword and used it to wreak havoc in Alfheimr (7). Saddened but resolute, the locals were forced to unravel the enchantment that had reanimated the child (8). As he grieved for his son a second time, Calivan realized some knowledge should be forbidden (9). No longer trusting his own ability to resist the temptation to use dark powers for his own benefit, he passed the Sword on to King Oberon for safekeeping (10).

Ace of Swords

Inquiry

Calivan, a Priest, insane with grief, dedicated himself to the process of inquiry in order to discover a means of bringing his wife, Isovel, back to life. In time, he became obsessed with inquiry, demanding to know even those things the gods had, in their wisdom, declined to reveal to the Elves. Here, as his dark studies progress, the Sword of Consciousness appears – perhaps to distract him.

Calivan's inquiries take place in a secret chamber; here, that chamber represents the need to withdraw in order to think clearly. Glowing script surrounds Calivan – a symbol of the limits of knowledge. What you don't know can often be far more important that what you do know – so remember to consider both.

The Ace of Swords represents an opportunity to ask a question that needs asking, to discover a fact that needs to be revealed, or to slice through debate and make a final decision. Inquiry is not meant to be an end in itself – instead, it's a process that should convey you forward to decisive and well-informed action.

Questions to Consider: What do you need to know? How can you go from debate to decision? What question are you avoiding right now?

Two of Swords
Choice

When the Dark Elves learned that Calivan was in possession of the Sword of Consciousness, they sent an agent to steal it from him. The Dark Elf broke into Calivan's home, took Calivan's son hostage, and demanded the Sword in exchange for sparing the boy's life.

Calivan, having taken responsibility for the Sword, faced a terrible choice. Holding on to the Sword would cost Galibrech his life ... but handing the Sword over to the Dark Elves would place a powerful object in the hands of the enemy.

Decision, decisions. If you've drawn this card, you likely face a choice between two equally pleasant (or unpleasant) options. The only way to move from deliberation to action is to review what you value. Once you're certain about what matters most, you'll be able to make this choice with ease.

Questions to Consider: What do I value most? How do my values inform my choices? What does my "gut" tell me to do in this situation?

Three of Swords

Consequence

Calivan chose to protect the Sword of Consciousness ... but that decision cost him the life of his only son. When Calivan took on the role of the Sword's protector, he could not have foreseen this outcome. Even so, in a very real way, the moment he laid hands on the Sword, his son was marked for death.

Decisions have consequences. The shield hanging over Calivan recalls a more familiar version of this card, linking this moment to heartbreak and disappointment. In this illustration, the boy, Galibrech, literally embodies the consequences of Calivan's choice.

If you've drawn this card, you're likely experiencing the consequences of a decision you've recently made. These consequences cannot always be anticipated. They may please us; they may not. They may be beneficial; they may not be. How you respond to a consequence is up to you ... but be aware, of course, that this decision, too, will have its consequences.

Questions to Consider: What do I want to have happen? What consequences would I prefer to avoid? When consequences come my way, what's the most mature way to deal with them?

Four of Swords

Stillness

Eventually, Calivan can no longer resist the temptation to use the Sword of Consciousness to bring his son back to life. Calivan has already accessed the forbidden knowledge; all that remains is to use that knowledge to trigger the Sword's enormous power and use it for selfish goals.

The rune above Calivan's head represents the principle of single-minded focus; something you would do well to apply in your current situation. The book in Calivan's hand represents the knowledge accessed through dedicated meditation. In your case, you may find that withdrawing and looking within helps you achieve your goal more quickly.

On the altar, Galibrech is arranged as a sacrifice would be – a reminder that dedication to meditation and transcendence often requires the sacrifice of precious moments that could be spent in other pursuits. The good news? Time spent listening to that "still, small voice within" often pays huge benefits later on.

Questions to Consider: How might silent meditation hold the key to my situation? What would I have to set aside in order to achieve clarity and mental focus?

Five of Swords

Chaos

The resurrected Galibrech lives and breathes, but as a creature animated by selfish motives, he is no longer the sweet, gentle Elf he was before. Here, the consequences of Calivan's actions spread far beyond the reality of personal sorrow and suffering, and waves of chaos disrupt the peace and well-being of innocent people.

When we no longer feel a connection with those around us ... when our own selfish needs become the sole basis for our morality ... when our every decision is colored by twisted logic ... chaos results. In this state, we are unable to think clearly or make positive progress (and we'd do well to retreat to the stillness of the Four).

Right now, you may be reeling from some injustice. Alternatively, because you may be so immersed in your own biased point of view, you cannot take rational action. Whatever the case: your judgment is severely impaired. Before you get hurt (and before you hurt someone else) step back, calm yourself, and get back in touch with reality.

Questions to Consider: What biases color my judgment? How can I calm my thoughts? What can I do to regain a sense of focus and peace?

Six of Swords

Protection

Six is the number of collaboration and cooperation; Swords is the suit of logic and decision-making. Just prior to this moment, the people of Alfheimr have been forced to make a collective decision banning the reanimated Galibrech – a desperate move, made in the best interest of all the city's citizens.

In other words, their collaboration has led them to define a threat and protect themselves from it. In this image, a city Elder (firm, but never vengeful) bans both Calivan and Alberich from Alfheimr. Calivan is distraught, but Galibrech lacks the capacity to be repentant or sorrowful.

If you've drawn this card, you are being advised to consult with others, identify a common problem, and outline a plan to protect yourself from dire or painful consequences. There is a need to "circle the wagons," see to your own safety, and make decisions now that insulate you from consequences that, today, are still on the horizon.

Questions to Consider: What other people are willing to take action in my best interest? What decisions, made today, would save me pain and suffering tomorrow?

Seven of Swords

Deceit

Calivan, struggles to meditate, hoping the pretense of a meditative pose will have a calming effect. Meanwhile, Galibrech takes the Sword of Consciousness in hand and sneaks away. This card, then, makes reference to two distinct activities: struggling to synchronize your actions and thoughts ... and acting in secret to achieve personal gain.

If you are normally a person who is prone to action, this card may well point to a need to pause, reflect, and meditate on your plans. You're most successful when your outer actions are aligned with inner goals. As long as you're "of two minds," you're not just deceiving others ... you're deceiving yourself.

The Seven of Swords may also suggest that there are others – apparently allies – who are secretly working against you. This resistance may be active, or it may come in the form of subtle sabotage: thinking negative thoughts, reinforcing bad behaviors, or enabling you to continue on a self-destructive path.

Questions to Consider: What people work against me by discouraging positive growth? How can I bring my own actions in alignment with my inner thoughts?

Eight of Swords

Restriction

Galibrech, carrying the Sword of Consciousness, returns to the city and wreaks havoc. The locals have no choice; in order to protect themselves from his persistent treachery, they must do more than restrict his freedom. In the end, their only recourse is to end the dark enchantment that perpetuates his life.

If you have drawn the Eight of Swords, you are facing some kind of limitation or restriction. Choices are limited. Options have dried up. You may feel trapped, tied down, or surrounded. For you, moving on may well be a matter of re-evaluating your situation, changing your goals, and revising your course of action.

It is also possible that restriction is a strategy you need to employ. If you feel torn in several directions at once, it may be time to limit your to-do list. If you can't decide which of several options to try, it may be time to go with one – any one – just to simplify your life.

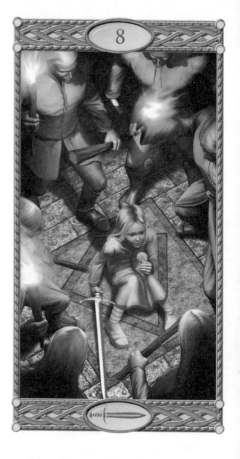

Questions to Consider: How can "cutting back" simplify my situation? What can I do to change course, radically change my thinking, or "think outside the box?"

Nine of Swords

Resignation

Here, a weary Calivan prays at the grave of Galibrech. The decisions that cost him his son are in the past and cannot be reversed. The verdicts of the people of Alfheimr have been enacted, and they cannot be revised. All that remains, at this point, is to accept what has been decided ... and deal with it as best he can.

Significantly, Calivan no longer holds or wields the Sword of Consciousness; instead, it has been strapped to his back for easy transport. In your own case, it's time to put rationalization and circular thought aside. Thinking or worrying about this situation further won't help you. By accepting what is, you'll embrace reality and begin to move on.

The Nine of Swords suggests a need for realistic thinking. Instead of struggling to change it, consider the benefits of accepting who and where you are. What might happen if you were to dedicate all that "worry energy" into actions designed to make the most of what your situation really is?

Questions to Consider: How does worry or over-thinking complicate my situation? What can I do to see the situation more clearly ... and embrace it?

Ten of Swords

Resolution

Based on his experiences, Calivan realizes he cannot be trusted with the power of the Sword of Consciousness. As a result, he knows he must abandon his post as guardian ... and so he turns the sword over to young King Oberon. The King, knowing the weapon's history, doesn't take this decision lightly.

Logic and clear thinking are powerful tools, but they can only carry you so far. There comes a point when decisions must be made and right action taken ... and you've reached that point. The Ten of Swords suggests that, like Calivan, you know the right thing to do. All that remains is for you to resolve to do it!

After struggling so long to make up your mind, you will find that making a decision and moving forward frees enormous energy. It's very much in your best interest to trust your instincts, make a choice, and move forward – even if doing so means giving up a post, position, or person you once felt honored to possess.

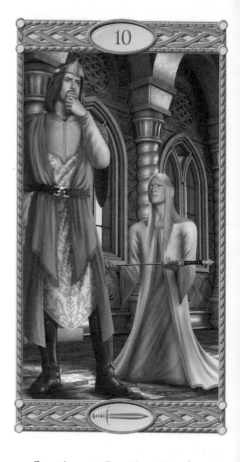

Questions to Consider: How have I been using the decision-making process as a means of procrastination? What external action can I take to show an internal decision has been made?

Page of Swords

Ignorance

Poor Galibrech makes the perfect Page of Swords. Here, seen before his reanimation, he finds himself drawn to new information ... but lacks the intelligence and experience to know how to interact properly with the world around him. As a result, he makes bad decisions – some of which have potential to produce painful complications.

The Page of Swords frequently refers to someone who is just beginning to make decisions ... and who, by virtue of inexperience or ignorance, is making some problematic choices. Watching this struggle can be difficult ... but children shielded from being "stung" occasionally never learn to run from angry bees.

The card may also suggest a strategy you need to employ: recognizing your own inexperience or ignorance. If you lack information to make a good choice, ask some questions. Do some research. Consult with others. If you're too proud to admit what you don't know, you may suffer consequences far worse than a simple sting.

Questions to Consider: How can I help an inexperienced friend make better choices? How can I improve my own choices by drawing on advice?

Knight of Swords

Agenda

Unseen, a Dark Elf lurks outside Calivan's window. Though Calivan has done everything he can to provide adequate protection for his family, his actions have attracted the attention of forces with ruthless agendas of their own. Even now, as father and son play together, the Dark Elves prepare to take action on their own behalf.

Knights are cards of action; Swords are the suit of decision-making and thought. This card, then, often points to someone who is thinking carefully about a plan designed to cater to his own best interests. This is a bit selfish, but it's something everyone does. You'd do well to remember that everyone has an agenda.

Your success in this situation may depend on defining your own agenda ... or learning to listen for and recognize the agendas of others. Consider your situation from alternative points of view. If you succeed, who profits? If you fail, who rejoices? These are the questions that will reveal agendas ... and protect you from those who would serve themselves at your expense.

Questions to Consider: What is my own agenda? Who else is involved in my situation – and what outcomes are they working for?

Queen of Swords

Memory

Here, in happier times, we see Galibrech with Isovel, his mother. She passes away before our story begins, but her influence – an echo of this perfect moment – persists throughout our story. Though she lives only in memory, she plays a powerful role in the story of the Sword. To understand her part better, you need only follow the trail of dandelions from card to card.

This card reminds you to be aware that facts and figures alone are not the only forces that influence our choices. For all our pretense of objectivity, memories – forged by emotional and unreasonable associations – all too often govern our decisions (even if only on a subconscious level).

The Queen of Swords, then, may point to anyone whose memory shapes your present actions, or it may suggest that someone you know is being driven by emotional memories instead of pure reason. Alternatively, it might suggest that the solution you seek will be found in your memory – and not in your mind.

Questions to Consider: What would a role model from my past do? What memory might be driving or complicating the situation I'm in?

King of Swords

Decisiveness

Here, Calivan tosses his book of forbidden knowledge into the fire. This decisive action, taken as a result of all he has experienced, cannot make amends for all that has happened – but it is an action taken with an eye toward a better, brighter future.

The King of Swords points to someone who is empowered to render final, decisive verdicts. This is a person who does not hesitate to speak his mind, offer opinions, and move forward with absolute confidence. His or her strength is rooted in an ability to "cut loose" anything or anyone who interferes with success.

Alternatively, the King of Swords may represent a strategy you should employ. If you are not moving forward as quickly as you hoped, it may be time to "cut loose" some of the encumbrances that limit your success. You should also examine your own thoughts. Can you take control and move forward by ferreting out self-defeating ideas that limit your options?

Questions to Consider: Who is the most decisive person I know? How can I be more like that person? What thoughts might be keeping me from decisive action?

The Suit of Discs
Fadonne and the Disc of Desire

Fadonne hated hard work, and resented having to gather nuts and berries to sell in the family store. One morning, while daydreaming of riches instead of doing her chores, she was shocked to see a spectral hand pointing to a shiny silver Disc lying on the dew-kissed grass (1).

A Dark Elf merchant offered Fadonne a small fortune for the Disc, but she refused, hoping to earn even more by placing it up for auction (2). But when Fadonne brought the Disc home, her brother Austafel and her sister Tristolae strongly disagreed over the price the Disc should bring (3). Tired of the argument, Fadonne buried the Disc for safekeeping (4), but by the time the family came to an agreement and she returned to retrieve the treasure, it was gone (5).

Consoled by her sister, Tristolae, Fadonne repented of her greed (6). The next day, on the market road, she met Bildr, a Dwarf who insisted he had purchased the Disc fairly from a young Elf who resembled Fadonne (7). Fadonne, feeling their meeting was fateful, agreed to work in Bildr's mines to earn the money to buy back the Disc (8). Over time, she became a hard and efficient worker, and, ultimately, she earned more than enough to purchase the Disc (9).

Once she possessed the Disc again, she realized she now preferred the true rewards of honest work over the imaginary riches of her daydreams. Rather than keep the disk for herself, she passed it on to King Oberon for safekeeping (10).

Ace of Discs

Opportunity

In this image, Fadonne discovers the Disc of Desire. The shock of discovery prompts her to spill her basket of berries and nuts. This is, of course, a metaphor: along with the potential benefits they bring, sudden opportunities almost always have some potential to "upset the apple cart" and disrupt business as usual.

When you draw the Ace of Discs, you are about to be on the receiving end of a financial or physical opportunity. This could manifest in any number of ways: a chance to improve your health, a chance to become more physically fit, an offer of a raise, or even a possible change in career.

If drawn when looking for a solution to a problem, the Ace of Discs often indicates the need to spend money or make physical changes. You might find yourself revising a budget, juggling funds, walking to work instead of driving, or electing to purchase healthy food instead of a greasy hamburger and French fries.

Questions to Consider: How do I feel about money? How can I take best advantage of the physical and financial opportunities that come my way?

Two of Discs

Appraisal

In this image, a Dark Elf – a symbolic figure associated with repressed feelings throughout Elven literature – tries to convince Fadonne to sell her newfound treasure. He offers her a substantial sum, but Fadonne, uncertain about the value and purpose of the Disc, rejects his offer.

Drawing the Two of Discs suggests that you are in the process of weighing your options – deciding, through the process of appraisal, what you truly value. Fadonne eventually decides that the Disc in her hand is worth more than a swarthy stranger's too-earnest offer. In your case: should you go with "the sure thing" ... or risk everything on a chance for more?

The answer, of course, lies in the value system you use to make such appraisals to begin with. If you value security, a conservative approach may be best. If you value growth and change, a more liberal (and less possessive) tact may be more appropriate. Once you get in touch with how and why your decisions are made, you'll find yourself making better decisions!

Questions to Consider: What do I really value? How do my values influence my decisions? What are my options "worth" in terms of short- and long-term value to me?

Three of Discs

Evaluation

The process of appraisal (see the entry for the Two of Discs) weighs several options against each other. But once an initial choice has been made and one option wins favor, evaluation is the process that determines the correctness and appropriateness of the selection you've made.

Problem is, different people evaluate different options in different ways. Here, Fadonne's family disagrees over the value and nature of the Disc of Desire. Her sister, Tristolae, (who evaluates opportunities based on their potential danger) wants the Disc out of the house; her brother, Austafel (motivated by greed), believes he should be appointed its guardian.

Having made an initial decision, it's time to practice due diligence: keep an eye on your progress, and, as you continue, pause from time to time to make sure you're achieving what you set out to achieve.

Questions to Consider: When have I stopped to evaluate how well I'm doing? What criteria will be used to judge the value and merit of my work?

Four of Discs

Preservation

Fadonne, unable to part with the Disc and unwilling to hand it over to her brother, decides to hide it by burying it deep in the earth. She's so focused on preserving her treasure, she fails to notice that her actions are being monitored from afar. Like most secrets, the location of Fadonne's hiding place proves all too easy to discover!

In burying the Disc, Fadonne is attempting to preserve her own power over it. All too often, a focus on preservation leads to greed, and greed – like any strong emotion – unbalances us. The tighter we cling to our secrets, the more obvious our true natures become!

In your situation, one of two things is needed. If you are over-indulging – overeating or over-spending – it's time to preserve your health and wealth by cutting back. If you are lacking something, it's time to abandon your poverty mentality, treat yourself well, and change your energy by letting the wealth of the Universe flow through you.

Questions to Consider: What would I fight to preserve? What things in my life don't merit preservation?

Five of Discs

Poverty

When Fadonne and her brother, Austafel, return to the hiding place, Fadonne (but not Austafel!) is shocked to find her treasure has been stolen. The hole in the ground is a symbol for the hole we feel in our hearts when we lose something precious – and a reminder that some things are so precious, no physical compensation can ease the pain of their loss.

Too often, the loss of material goods or physical health leads us into a trap: a poverty of spirit. A quiet voice begins to tell us that we don't deserve good fortune, and we, already defeated, begin to believe it. That negative energy attracts more loss and misfortune, and, in time, we are spiraling downward.

Rather than focus on what you don't have, focus on what you do. The Five of Wands is a sobering reminder that you have more resources than you think – and that accessing them is usually a matter of putting your losses behind you. Meanwhile, if all is currently sweetness and sunshine – plan ahead; this card often suggests "rainy days" are coming!

Questions to Consider: What can I do about my "poverty mentality?" What resources are waiting for me to discover them?

Six of Discs

Charity

Realizing her loss – and the loss of wealth it represents for her family – Fadonne repents. Austafel responds with aloofness ... but Tristolae is quick to comfort Fadonne and suggest that there are better times ahead. For now, Fadonne is consumed with grief – in this case, though, grief is an indicator of a change in her basic character.

When you're devastated, the smallest gesture – a smile, a hand on your shoulder, a simple gift, a warm meal – can make all the difference in your outlook and attitude. These acts of charity bind people together, building unbreakable bonds. Those who contribute are rewarded; those who hold back hurt no one but themselves.

In your situation, some charitable action is called for. To encourage success, make a small gift or donation. To heal yourself, forgive someone. If facing a problem too large for you to handle personally, ask others for the support you need.

Questions to Consider: How can I be an example of charity in action? How can I comfort or aid others? What comfort or aid do I need to ask for?

Seven of Discs

Redemption

On the Market Road, Fadonne stumbles across Bildr, a shrewd and profit-minded Dwarf. When Bildr proves he purchased the Disc of Desire from a young man he says might well have been Fadonne's twin, she understands her situation in a new light. Rather than throw a tantrum or sink back into grief, she asks how she might earn the Disc back.

By refusing to blame others for her situation, Fadonne redeems herself and takes a step onto the road of independence and true power. Faced with a difficult situation, she figures out a way to remedy her problems using nothing more than the resources the gods have given her. In doing so, she transforms herself from victim into heroine.

When you draw the Seven of Discs, this is often an indication of a need to think carefully about the actions you should take to make a difficult situation better. No more waiting around or blaming others! If you want your world to be a better place, it's time for you to consider what *you* can do.

Questions to Consider: How can I redeem myself by taking action on my own behalf? In what way have I been playing the victim?

Eight of Discs
Worth

Neither Bildr nor his twin brother, Boldr, thought a weak, sheltered girl like Fadonne would linger more than a day in their mines. Fadonne soon proved her worth, though, by laboring long hours, refusing to quit, and boosting the brother's profits beyond their wildest dreams.

The Eight of Discs recommends, then, that you prove your worth by applying yourself. Now is the time to work hard, keep your nose to the grindstone, and make a special effort to achieve what you've set out to achieve. In doing so, you will not only increase your worth in the eyes of others ... you'll also feel better about yourself.

This hard work will be easier to do if you keep your mind focused on the goal ... and what it will be worth to you, when you achieve it. With a little single-minded application of effort, you'll have something worth celebrating in very short order.

Questions to Consider: How good am I at hard work? To what extent am I making my very best effort?

Nine of Discs

Reward

Having successfully completed the tasks set before her, Fadonne receives a fair wage for her work. Because she exceeded his expectations, Bildr not only gives Fadonne the Disc he promised ... but several bags of jewels, too! This rewards her good effort and balances the karmic scales, as well.

Boldr, not quite as free-hearted as Bildr, secretly holds back a portion of the reward for himself. The greedy are always with us; ultimately, though, we choose whether or not we will allow their actions to deprive us of the joy we feel when we know we've given our best.

In your situation, be open to a reward, and accept whatever is offered with grace and good sense. If you are in a position to evaluate the work of others, be as free with praise and rewards as circumstances allow. If you are having trouble getting motivated, try focusing on the rewards you'll earn when your work is complete.

Questions to Consider: What kind of reward would really excite me? How willing am I to work for rewards? How freely do I give them?

Ten of Discs

Restoration

Fadonne, realizing that the Disc of Desire is too valuable for any one person to own or control, passes her hard-won prize on to young King Oberon for safe-keeping. In doing so, she restores the balance of power in the kingdom.

In your situation, it's likely that something needs to be restored. Look for an opportunity to right an old wrong, forgive a debt, or repair a broken friendship. Rather than buy something new, consider how an existing resource could be reconfigured or refitted to serve a new purpose.

Alternatively, you may find yourself in need of restoration. You can achieve this easily by visiting old friends, indulging in some physical pleasure, or giving yourself permission to purchase a substantial but reasonable gift for yourself.

Questions to Consider: How can I mend what's been broken? What actions can I take that would make this situation better immediately?

Page of Discs

Attachment

Early in the story, Fadonne embodies the energy of the Page of Discs. She lacks the experience and wisdom needed to handle financial and physical issues with grace. Because she cannot understand the value of what she possesses, she is unnaturally and illogically attached to it.

This card is very likely to point to someone who shares these qualities: a young person who is careless with money or unconcerned about his or her physical health. Alternately, this card may point to someone who is just beginning to be fiscally and physically responsible: a person starting an overdue exercise program or diet or a college student opening a first bank account.

The Page of Discs may also represent a strategy worth trying: spending your money on some new thing, trying a physical activity you've neglected or dismissed, or allowing yourself to indulge in a forbidden treat.

Questions to Consider: How can I get past unhealthy attachments to physical goods or unhealthy foods? What can I do to handle my money more responsibly?

Knight of Discs

Selfishness

Austafel, Fadonne's brother, noted the location of her treasure and, much later, returned to steal it for himself. Like his sister, he didn't understand the value of the Disc; unlike his sister, he was willing to take action on his own behalf and sell the Disc to meet his own selfish needs.

The Knight of Discs is a card of action. When the opportunity for an investment arises, the Knight takes it. When there is a chance to spend money, the Knight whips out his wallet without hesitation. Channel his energy with care, as everything you're offered may not be worth buying.

When you take action on your own behalf, there is a danger of being called (or actually becoming) selfish. Weigh your motives carefully; only you can know whether your actions are driven by an impure agenda. When you draw this card, don't hesitate to move forward ... but keep a level head about you, particularly with respect to physical or financial decisions.

Questions to Consider: How greedy am I? To what extent are my plans motivated by selfishness? When is selfishness bad? Is it ever good?

Queen of Discs

Bounty

Fadonne's sister, Tristolae, rejects the Disc of Desire outright because she knows she and her family can generate enough wealth on their own. Unlike her brother and sister, Tristolae has an abundance mentality ... and, as a result, her own life is full of blessing and bounty.

The Queen of Discs invites you to believe, if only for a moment, that you have everything you need. In addition, she encourages you to believe that you can have all you want. Her process is simple: "Ask, and you shall receive."

In your current situation, you'd do well to take her advice. Have a need? Picture it filled. Have a challenge? Picture it resolved. Have a dream? Picture it becoming a reality. If you lack Tristolae's physical and financial self-confidence, consider the value of acting as though you share her trust in the Universe!

Questions to Consider: What can I do to encourage an abundance mentality? How willing am I to ask for what I need? How much do I trust the universe to deliver it?

King of Discs

Stewardship

Bildr has a great deal of wealth at his disposal for one reason: he's a good steward of every penny the gods entrust to him. Bildr is the ultimate accountant, always aware of what's coming in, what's going out, and how hard his wealth is working for him.

In your situation, there's a need for this level of attention to financial or physical detail. The King of Discs recommends completing inventory, conducting audits, and balancing checkbooks. This is a time to put money in the bank, repay loans, and collect or forgive old debts.

On the physical end of the spectrum, The King of Discs reminds you to exercise regularly, get checkups on a regular basis, and pay special attention to diets. Borrow his willpower and determination, and you'll find yourself the recipient of great wealth – including some treasures money can't buy.

Questions to Consider: How can I be a better steward of what I've been given? What could I do to be a healthier, more responsible person?

Divination
With the Tarot of the Elves

The Tarot of the Elves may be used as you would any other Tarot deck: shuffling the cards, dealing them into a spread, and reading the cards based on your intuition, the meanings assigned in this book, or both.

The Elven Wisdom Spread

This spread, developed especially for use with this deck, draws on the archetypal energy of the Tarot of the Elves as a means of generating profound insights. Repeat it as often as needed, taking careful notes.

1) Within the Major or Minor Arcana, **find one card** you feel connects with or reflects the situation that has prompted this reading. Remove this card from the deck, designate it as "Card One," and place it face up on the table.

2) Shuffle the remaining cards.

3) Deal four additional face-down cards into the four compass points surrounding Card One, forming a simple cross:
– Card Two in the West
– Card Three in the North
– Card Four in the South
– Card Five in the East

4) Reveal Card Two. This card should reflect some aspect of your situation's past; you should recognize the reference very easily, if not immediately. If you connect with this card with your personal story, move on to the next step. If you cannot, collect all the cards but Card One, reshuffle, and repeat this step until Card Two does reflect some aspect of the past.

5) Reveal Card Three. This card represents the spiritual or archetypal lesson your current struggle is designed to teach you. Meditate on this card until you achieve a clear sense of the benefit you will receive as a result of working through your situation.

6) Reveal Card Four. This card represents the seed of the solution: the critical factor that, once identified, will allow you to turn the situation to your advantage. Write down at least four possible interpretations of this card before continuing.

7) Reveal Card Five. This card represents your first step on your personal "Hero's Journey" – one thing you can do today to move a little closer to your goal.

Finding Your Place in the Story

In addition to standard card divination with spreads, you may also find it useful to draw a single card from the shuffled deck. Finding that card within the deck and looking at the cards that come immediately after it may provide new insights into your personal story. For example: if you draw the Four of Coins, your situation may somehow involve an admirable but misguided effort to preserve something. The illustration on the Five of Coins may suggest a potential outcome you can avoid by changing your approach in the present.

With time and practice, you will quickly see parallels between Elven mythology and your own situation ... making it possible for you to anticipate future events and position yourself to take best advantage of whatever comes your way.